Quebec City 148

Bar Harbor 114

St. John's 162

the Bay of fundy 154

Halifax 158

PORTLAND 108

Portsmouth 104

Cambridge 100

PROVINCETOWN 88

BOSTON 94

Newport 76

NANTUCKET 84

PROVIDENCE 72

MARTHA'S VINEYARD 80

APOLLO
Harlem 28

Broadway 24

Lower Manhattan 18

Brooklyn 34

NORTH EAST

EDITED BY BARBARA IRELAND

The New York Times

HOURS
USA & CANADA
NORTHEAST

TASCHEN

Contents

Foreword

The Northeast is urban America at its most intense, frenetic, and exciting, with a metropolitan sprawl spreading for hundreds of miles down the Atlantic coast. It is also placid seaside-and-steeple villages in New England and history-saturated towns like Philadelphia or Princeton. And it holds the oldest settlements of Canada — Quebec City, Montreal, St. John's — all grown up and jammed with things to see and do.

In contrast to the widely spaced cities of the West, the travelers' landmarks in the Northeast seem close together, almost crowded, in a dense tapestry of color and activity so rich that it can feel intimidating. And it's true, of course — New York alone could occupy a visitor's attention for months on end. But in only a weekend, you might be able to delve deeper than you ever imagined.

A well-plotted itinerary makes all the difference, and this book lays out 31 of them, all updated or new, and all adapted from the weekly 36 Hours travel feature in The New York Times. From Newfoundland to New Jersey, they explore the possibilities of the Northeastern weekend trip.

Begin in New York, the first stop in North America for many a foreign traveler and the turf that Times writers know best. Five separate 36 Hours itineraries cover the city from Broadway to Brooklyn, with stops for theater and art, five-star restaurants and happening bars, Wall Street, Harlem culture, hipster hangouts, and a view of the Statue of Liberty from the Staten Island Ferry.

Take a trip south, to Philadelphia's landmarks of Benjamin Franklin and Rocky Balboa, or to the Victorian resort and birder's paradise of Cape May. Go inland to Cooperstown, the town where baseball and opera coexist, or to Burlington, where maple syrup and a green sensibility rule.

And there is all that territory to the north: historic, busy Boston and its intellectual suburb of Cambridge, home of Harvard and M.I.T.; seafaring New London and Portsmouth; the rocky Maine coast at Portland and Bar Harbor; Cape Cod and its offshore cousins, Martha's Vineyard and Nantucket.

Go mansion-touring in Newport or the Brandywine Valley; check out beaches and celebrity playgrounds in the Hamptons; ski at Mont Tremblant, Lake Placid, or Stowe. And in town after town, sample great shopping, good eating, and plenty of places to find live music or a quiet cocktail after dark.

The newspaper feature that gave birth to this book, 36 Hours, has been a reader favorite for more than a decade. Created as a guide to the weekend getaway, 36 Hours takes readers each week on a carefully researched, uniquely designed two-night excursion to an embraceable place. It outlines an experience that both identifies the high points of the destination and teases out its particular character.

In late 2011, The New York Times and TASCHEN published The New York Times 36 Hours: 150 Weekends in the U.S.A. & Canada, which gathered together 150 North American 36 Hours columns in one volume. In 2012, the decision was made to offer this trove of travel guidance in another format: as five regional books, each easily portable and particularly focused, to meet the needs of a traveler who wants to concentrate on one area at a time. You are reading now from one of the five; the others are devoted to the Southeast, the Midwest and Great Lakes, the Southwest and Rocky Mountains, and the West Coast including Alaska and Hawaii.

The work of hundreds of writers, photographers, graphic artists, designers, and editors, combining their talents over many years, has gone into 36 Hours. Each of them shares in its creation. In this book, their talents bring together two elements that fit happily together: northeastern North America and the great American weekend.

— BARBARA IRELAND, EDITOR

PAGE 2 Liberty lifts her lamp in New York Harbor.

PAGE 4 Bricks and cobblestones of Boston.

OPPOSITE Portland Head Light at Cape Elizabeth, Maine.

Tips for Using This Book

Plotting the Course: Travelers don't make their way through a region or a country alphabetically, and this book doesn't proceed that way, either. It begins in a major city emblematic of the region and winds from place to place the way a touring adventurer on a car trip might. An alphabetical index appears at the end of the book.

On the Ground: Every *36 Hours* follows a workable numbered itinerary, which is both outlined in the text and shown with corresponding numbers on a detailed destination map. The itinerary is practical: it really is possible to get from one place to the next easily and in the allotted time, although of course many travelers will prefer to take things at their own pace and perhaps take some of their own detours. Astute readers will notice that the "36" in *36 Hours* is elastic, and the traveler's agenda probably will be, too.

The Not So Obvious: The itineraries do not all follow exactly the same pattern. A restaurant for Saturday breakfast may or may not be recommended; after-dinner night life may be included or may not. The destination dictates, and so, to some extent, does the personality of the author who researched and wrote the article. In large cities, where it is impossible to see everything in a weekend, the emphasis is on the less expected discovery over the big, highly promoted attraction that is already well known.

Seasons: The time of year to visit is left up to the traveler, but in general, the big cities are good anytime; towns where snow falls are usually best visited in warm months, unless they are ski destinations; and summer heat is more or less endurable depending on the traveler's own tolerance. The most tourist-oriented areas are often seasonal—some of the sites featured in vacation towns may be closed out of season.

Your Own Agenda: This book is not a conventional guidebook. A *36 Hours* is meant to give a well-informed inside view of each place it covers, a selective summary that lets the traveler get to the heart of things in minimal time. Travelers who have more days to spend may want to use a *36 Hours* as a kind of nugget, supplementing it with the more comprehensive information available on bookstore shelves or on the locally sponsored Internet sites where towns and regions offer exhaustive lists of their attractions. Or, two or three of these itineraries can easily be strung together to make up a longer trip.

Updates: While all the stories in this volume were updated and fact-checked for publication in fall 2011, it is inevitable that some of the featured businesses and destinations will change in time. If you spot any errors in your travels, please feel free to send corrections or updates via email to 36hoursamerica@taschen.com. Please include "36 Hours Correction" and the page number in the subject line of your email to assure that it gets to the right person for future updates.

OPPOSITE Whiteface Mountain, where Olympic skiers raced.

THE BASICS

A brief informational box for the destination, called "The Basics," appears with each *36 Hours* article in this book. The box provides some orientation on transportation for that location, including whether a traveler arriving by plane should rent a car to follow the itinerary. "The Basics" also recommends three reliable hotels or other lodgings.

PRICES

Since hotel and restaurant prices change quickly, this book uses a system of symbols, based on 2011 United States dollars.

Hotel room, standard double:
Budget, under $100 per night: $
Moderate, $100 to $199: $$
Expensive, $200 to $299: $$$
Luxury, $300 and above: $$$$

Restaurants, dinner without wine:
Budget, under $15: $
Moderate, $16 to $24: $$
Expensive, $25 to $49: $$$
Very Expensive, $50 and up: $$$$

Restaurants, full breakfast, or lunch entree:
Budget, under $8: $
Moderate, $8 to $14: $$
Expensive, $15 to $24: $$$
Very Expensive, $25 and up: $$$$

New York City

In New York City, a continent opens its doors and urban renewal never stops. Someone new is always getting off the bus, train, or plane, some new idea is always catching fire, and the skyscrapers just keep on rising. If it's your first time in town, you'll feel the buzz — this is energy central for American culture. If you are returning after a couple of years away, change is what you'll find: crowds explore a hot new park, familiar landmarks have gotten face lifts, and the center of cool has shifted innumerable times (but it's probably still somewhere in Brooklyn). — BY AMY VIRSHUP

FRIDAY

1 *Get Your Tickets* 5 p.m.

The refurbished **Lincoln Center** (Broadway between 62nd and 63rd Streets; lincolncenter.org), includes not only a new fountain with 353 custom-made, computer-controlled nozzles, but a new visitors' center and ticketing space, the **David Rubenstein Atrium** (that's what you get when you give $10 million). The box office sells same-day discount tickets at 25 to 50 percent off regular prices, with a two-ticket-per-person limit, for the Metropolitan Opera, the New York Philharmonic, the New York City Ballet, and the City Opera. Check to see what's on and pick up a pair for tonight.

2 *Pre-theater Prix Fixe* 6 p.m.

Daniel Boulud's New York culinary empire now runs from the Bowery to the Upper East Side. Just across from Lincoln Center, his **Bar Boulud** (1900 Broadway near 64th Street; 212-595-0303; danielnyc.com; $$$) is the perfect perch for a pre-performance meal. Terrines, sliced meats, and cheeses (the last divided into categories like Bloomy, Stinky, and Old & Hard) are the heart of the menu, but there's also a three-course prix-fixe option that includes such classic choices as a salade niçoise, roasted chicken breast, and house-made ice cream or sorbet. For the full experience, sit at the

charcuterie bar, where the view includes fromage de tête Gilles Verot (that's headcheese for those who don't speak French). Afterward, grab a drink at the **Alice Tully Hall** lobby bar before curtain time at Lincoln Center.

SATURDAY

3 *Breakfast, Retro-Style* 10 a.m.

Find the **Standard Grill** at the base of the Standard Hotel (848 Washington Street at West 13th Street; 212-645-4100; thestandardgrill.com; $$). Despite the hotel's Brutalism-Meets-Miami-Beach exterior, the dining room is pure retro: a tile-vaulted ceiling, penny (as in real pennies) floor, red leather banquettes. The menu is pleasingly retro, too: warm cinnamon-and-sugar-crusted doughnuts made on the spot, for example, or ultra-sweet French toast with bananas and rum sauce.

4 *Upside of the Tracks* 11 a.m.

Just down the block at the corner of Gansevoort and Washington Streets are the southernmost stairs to the **High Line** (thehighline.org), the immensely popular linear park recently created on what was once an abandoned freight rail line. On a summer weekend thousands of people might be walking on it, but it's fun even in winter, when it has a quieter, almost derelict

OPPOSITE Manhattan at dusk.

RIGHT The Lake in Central Park. Weather permitting, rowboats can be rented during the summer from the Loeb Boathouse near Fifth Avenue and 72nd Street.

beauty, with bare tree limbs and the seed heads of grasses swaying in the wind off the Hudson.

5 *Brooklyn Browsing* 1 p.m.

Once known as the city of churches, Brooklyn these days might be called the borough of boutiques. For a taste, take the 2/3 or 4/5 subway train to Borough Hall and walk to Court Street in the Cobble

ABOVE The High Line rises above Chelsea along a former elevated train track.

BELOW Foot traffic at Herald Square, where Broadway meets Sixth Avenue in Midtown Manhattan.

Hill neighborhood. At tiny **Fork & Pencil** (221a Court; 718-488-8855; forkandpencil.com) look for imaginative housewares, toys, and antiques. The proceeds go to support local charities. **Papél New York** (225 Court; 718-422-0255; papelnewyork.com) sells sleek paper goods, including sheets of wrapping paper that will class up even the smallest of gifts. Need to refuel? The Stumptown Coffee at **Cafe Pedlar** (210 Court; 718-855-7129; cafepedlar.com) is roasted nearby in Red Hook, and you can pick up a bag of Hair Bender blend beans along with your espresso. Or stop at the **Chocolate Room** (269 Court; 718-246-2600; thechocolateroombrooklyn.com) for homemade chocolate caramel popcorn.

6 *New Yorkers at Play* 6 p.m.

You've hiked the new park; now stroll the old standby. To see the real New Yorkers at play in **Central Park** late on a Saturday afternoon, enter

well north of the touristy horse-drawn hansom cabs and schlock art vendors on Central Park South. Here's one good route: Use the 77th Street entrance from Central Park West (across from the American Museum of Natural History) and wind your way south along the Lake, detouring to Strawberry Fields if you're a John Lennon fan, and then east to Bethesda Fountain. Climb the stairs, walk south on the Mall (look out for tango dancers), and wind your way to Columbus Circle. The paths are easy to get lost on, so take a map or keep one handy on your cellphone (Google's isn't bad).

7 *Seafood on the Park* 8 p.m.

Sleek and highly polished, **Marea** (240 Central Park South; 212-582-5100; marea-nyc.com; $$$), just east of Columbus Circle, is like some movie version of New York except, yes, that really is a fallen mogul pitching new investors at the table next to yours. The menu is devoted to an Italian spin on fish. Share an order of the unctuous ricci (sea urchin, lardo, and sea salt draped bruschetta-like over toast), then choose among the crudo (raw fish), oysters, and antipasti.

ABOVE Columbus Circle, just off Central Park.

RIGHT The Metropolitan Opera House at Lincoln Center. Discounted same-day tickets can be purchased at the David Rubenstein Atrium.

For a main course you can get a whole fish roasted or sautéed, then choose your sauce and side dish.

8 *Cocktails and Codes* 10 p.m.

If you're talking cocktails in New York these days, you need to know two words: speakeasy and artisanal. In dark, hidden spots, behind hard-to-find entrances, bartenders are mixing up concoctions with names like Corpse Reviver No. 2 (gin, Cointreau, Lillet Blanc, lemon, and absinthe) that only seem

old-fashioned. That particular drink was assembled by the garter-sleeved bartenders at **Little Branch** (20 Seventh Avenue South at Leroy Street; 212-929-4360). Cash only.

SUNDAY

9 *Comfort Breakfast* 10 a.m.

The name is an oxymoron and the kitchen is probably smaller than yours, but **Little Giant** (85

OPPOSITE An exhibition at the New Museum of Contemporary Art.

ABOVE Economy Candy on the Lower East Side.

BELOW Speakeasy-style cocktails are served up at Little Branch in the West Village.

Orchard Street at the corner of Broome; 212-226-5047; littlegiantnyc.com; $$-$$$) turns out slightly refined comfort food that has crowds piling up on the sidewalks of the gentrifying Lower East Side. Little Giant serves a Trucker's Breakfast, but the bacon with it will be hand-sliced and the mushrooms cremini. Weekend brunch is cash only.

10 *Art Under Construction* 11 a.m.

The anchor of the Lower East Side art scene is the **New Museum of Contemporary Art** (235 Bowery at Prince Street; 212-219-1222; newmuseum.org), designed by the Japanese firm Sanaa to look like a

series of off-kilter boxes, which opened to raves in 2007. Examine the art inside and then stroll outside to look for more. A growing number of storefronts in the Lower East Side are studios where artists and gallerists with big ambitions work small for now.

11 *Sugar Rush* 1 p.m.

A giant Gummi rat. How New York is that? You can pick one up to take home, along with giant pixie sticks, wax fangs, Mallo Cups, and classics like Hot

Tamales and Mike and Ikes at **Economy Candy** (108 Rivington Street; 212-254-1531; economycandy.com). Crammed with what seems like every candy bar ever known, plus hard candies by the pound, nuts, and dried fruits, it's a playground for the sugar-obsessed.

ABOVE A view of New York Harbor.

OPPOSITE New York's iconic Flatiron Building, at the confluence of Fifth Avenue and Broadway.

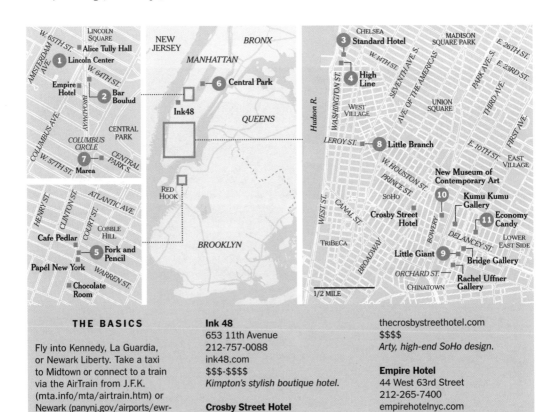

THE BASICS

Fly into Kennedy, La Guardia, or Newark Liberty. Take a taxi to Midtown or connect to a train via the AirTrain from J.F.K. (mta.info/mta/airtrain.htm) or Newark (panynj.gov/airports/ewr-airtrain.html). Taxis are plentiful. The subway is convenient and safe.

Ink 48
653 11th Avenue
212-757-0088
ink48.com
$$$-$$$$
Kimpton's stylish boutique hotel.

Crosby Street Hotel
79 Crosby Street
212-226-6400

thecrosbystreethotel.com
$$$$
Arty, high-end SoHo design.

Empire Hotel
44 West 63rd Street
212-265-7400
empirehotelnyc.com
$$$
Steps from Lincoln Center.

Lower Manhattan

Welcome to Lower Manhattan. You're already behind schedule. Here in the pre-grid city, where Broadway started as a path and Wall Street once really had a wall, the streets may be old but the pace is quick and the outlook is young. Bond traders and bohemians, tai chi practitioners and adventurous just-minted college grads are all sprinkled into the mix. Was it really just a decade or so ago that people wondered if the area would ever recover from the shock of the attacks that took down the World Trade Center? Since then the pace of development has only intensified. Thirty-six hours seems far too little time to cover it all. But it's a great start. — BY ARIEL KAMINER

FRIDAY

1 *Hang Out* 3:30 p.m.

On a tiny platform 23 feet off the ground, every natural impulse tells you to stay away from the edge. But Jonah, a rather dreamy trapeze instructor, tells you to lean over it — way over it — and so you lean. Then he tells you to bend your knees and jump off. And so, against all reason, you jump. What follows is something close to flying, accompanied by the incomparable sensation of zoom and the sound, perhaps, of your own giddy scream. That first step is a doozy all right, but the odd collection of charming teachers at the **Trapeze School New York** (Pier 40, Hudson River Park opposite Houston Street; 917-797-1872; trapezeschool.com; $57 for a two-hour beginner class, plus $22 registration fee) make it fun. The school has several locations; this one, open in the warm months, sits right on the river, with peerless views of the Statue of Liberty and the skyline. What better way to situate yourself in Lower Manhattan than while hanging from your knees and swinging a 70-degree arc?

2 *Footing the Bill* 6 p.m.

Feel wobbly? Time for acupressure massage at the **Fishion Herb Center** (107 Mott Street; 212-966-8771; fishionherbcenter.com), a cramped

warren of fluorescent-lighted cubicles that's far, indeed, from the Swiss apple stem cell facials of uptown spas, not just in ambience but (delightfully) in price. Settle into a cracked old wing chair while a Chinese masseur bears down on the tip of your fourth toe, or the area right inside your heel, tiny spots said to correspond to precise parts of the body. Check the laminated chart and note that he's put his hands on not only your "liver" and "spleen" but also places — hello! — not fit to name in a family newspaper. What's the standard tip for that?

3 *Bridge to the 19th Century* 8 p.m.

Depending on whose story you believe, the **Bridge Café** (279 Water Street; 212-227-3344; bridgecafenyc.com; $$-$$$) may be the city's oldest drinking establishment, tracing its ancestry to 1794. It wears its history lightly, with a low-key New American menu and friendly setting (seared diver scallops; grilled petite lamb chops). After dinner you can wander the almost ridiculously picturesque streets just south of the Brooklyn Bridge (but north of the dreaded South Street Seaport mall), cobblestone alleys right out of a Walt Whitman poem. Or, if you haven't seen it, walk a few blocks west to the World Trade Center site and take some time to ponder.

OPPOSITE Brunch at Blaue Gans, a Viennese-style coffee house on Duane Street.

RIGHT Open since 1794, the Bridge Cafe on Water Street at the foot of the Brooklyn Bridge.

4 *Admission to the Bar* 10 p.m.

Lower Manhattan is also the seat of the city government, so fight the lure of yet another *Law & Order* rerun and go see the real thing in action. The gritty night session of New York Criminal Court, at 100 Centre Street, is open to the public, but applause and/or booing is strongly discouraged. Afterward, go to **Forlini's** (93 Baxter Street; 212-349-6779) to have a Scotch with the only team that always comes out on top: the lawyers. Or, take a short perp walk toward the Tombs, Lower Manhattan's very own jail, and find **Winnie's** (104 Bayard Street; 212-732-2384), a gloriously, garishly seedy dive bar where tough customers and painted ladies drink cocktails and sing karaoke into the morning.

SATURDAY

5 *Tai Chi Theater* 9 a.m.

Full-body exercise can be a great start to the day, especially when you're not the one doing it. Every morning in Chinatown's Columbus Park, old men, young students, and graceful women of a certain age gather in their own little groups to perform tai chi. Whatever its spiritual or physical benefits, it makes for beautiful spectacle, with everyone moving in perfectly choreographed slow motion, as though performing water ballet on land.

6 *Vienna Goods* 11 a.m.

By Saturday night, **Blaue Gans** (139 Duane Street; 212-571-8880; kg-ny.com; $$), an update on the classic Viennese coffee house, is a crowded scene restaurant. But at this hour it's peaceful, sunny, and oh so European, from the newspapers dangling from a bentwood rack to the soccer match on TV to the counter filled with pastries expressing principled dissent from American diet trends. Order some Wiener schnitzel the size of Poland or Kaiserschmarren (what might have been called French toast before the Franco-Prussian War) and enjoy the most elaborate coffee presentation since the days of the Habsburgs.

7 *Art and About* 1 p.m.

Big scary galleries and august museums may hardly take notice, but new cultural activity still thrives amid Lower Manhattan's condo sales offices. TriBeCa is sprinkled with galleries, among them **apexart** (291 Church Street; 212-431-5270; apexart.org), a small nonprofit space that emphasizes group shows with a political theme; **Art in General** (79 Walker Street; 212-219-0473; artingeneral.org), an old-timer by comparison, which commissions work that might not find a home in other venues; and **Ethan Cohen Gallery** (14 Jay Street; 212-625-1250; ecfa.com), which specializes in contemporary Chinese art.

OPPOSITE The view of Lower Manhattan from across the East River, at Brooklyn Bridge Park in Dumbo.

RIGHT The Staten Island Ferry cruises by the Statue of Liberty at dusk.

BELOW Tourists gather around the Wall Street Bull along Broadway in the Financial District.

8 *And Staten Island, Too* 5 p.m.

Is there any greater cliché than a sunset ride on the **Staten Island Ferry**? No, and so what? Grab a beer at the snack bar and a spot on the bow and toast Lady Liberty standing among all the tribes she spawned: dudes in fake Gucci, biddies back from the Met, and, on one visit, a lumbering Goth goddess hiding behind elaborate facial tattoos. (Ferries run 24 hours; siferry.com; fare, free.)

9 *Dine and Wine* 9 p.m.

TriBeCa has more than its share of multistarred restaurants, but they're booked, expensive, and awfully serious. Take the bistro route without denying yourself the white tablecloths by dining at the **Harrison** (355 Greenwich Street, at Harrison Street; 212-274-9310; theharrison.com/harrison.php; $$-$$$). Expect modern American fare like seared skate wing or updated twists on roasted chicken, and plan to linger a while.

10 *Sofia on the Hudson* Midnight

If you can choose only one Bulgarian hipster bar this weekend, **Mehanata** is the way to go. This freakish little hybrid is at Broadway and Canal (113 Ludlow Street; 212-625-0981; mehanata.com), but at times it feels like a different country, or planet. The crowd is a mix of cute college girls, sullen artists, and burly Eastern Europeans — with the odd whirling dervish thrown in for good measure. As a D.J. spins

something trendy, everyone drinks and dances, and soon enough the night slides over the edge into genuinely weird terrain. Food is available but in no way advisable.

SUNDAY

11 *Why Is It So Bright?* 11 a.m.
There's something about dancing tabletop with a band of crazed Bulgarian hedonists that changes a person—but how, and for how long, it's best not to ask. Much better plan: brunch at **Smorgas Chef** on Stone Street, a pretty cobblestone lane in the

Financial District (53 Stone Street; 212-422-3500; smorgas.com/index_wallstreet.htm; $$). Bring a stack of newspapers but do not read them. Instead, treat yourself to smoked salmon eggs Benedict, administer frequent doses of coffee, and ignore the ringing in your head. It will subside eventually. It has to.

ABOVE Stone Street, said by some to be the oldest paved street in New York City. Today it's a spot for bars, lofts, and Sunday coffee.

OPPOSITE Flying high at Trapeze School New York.

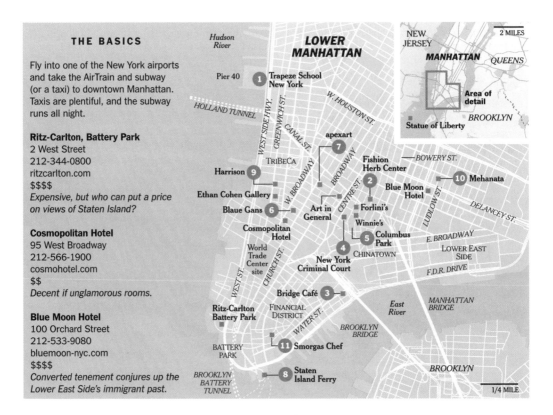

THE BASICS

Fly into one of the New York airports and take the AirTrain and subway (or a taxi) to downtown Manhattan. Taxis are plentiful, and the subway runs all night.

Ritz-Carlton, Battery Park
2 West Street
212-344-0800
ritzcarlton.com
$$$$
Expensive, but who can put a price on views of Staten Island?

Cosmopolitan Hotel
95 West Broadway
212-566-1900
cosmohotel.com
$$
Decent if unglamorous rooms.

Blue Moon Hotel
100 Orchard Street
212-533-9080
bluemoon-nyc.com
$$$$
Converted tenement conjures up the Lower East Side's immigrant past.

Broadway

Four plays in one weekend? Why not? On Broadway, the best of American theatrical talent comes together in 41 theaters within a tight cluster of walkable New York City blocks. The schedules are right, the marquees are bright, and the variety of the productions gives you plenty to choose from. Between shows, follow celebrity footsteps into some hangouts of the theater people and learn some Broadway history. This district has been home of the best (and worst) of what the New York stage has to offer for more than a century.
— BY MERVYN ROTHSTEIN

FRIDAY

1 *Ticket Strategy* 2 p.m.

Lengthy treatises have been written about how to get Broadway tickets. One option is to join the line at the discount **TKTS** booth at the north end of Times Square (tdf.org/tkts), sponsored by the nonprofit Theater Development Fund. The latest hits aren't likely to show up here, but good productions well into their runs may be available, and savings can be 25 percent to 50 percent. Lines form well before the booth opens at 3 p.m. Whether you buy at TKTS, pay full price at a theater box office, or book weeks ahead through **Telecharge** (telecharge.com) or **Ticketmaster** (ticketmaster.com), study the reviews and listings first. To span the Broadway experience, plan to see a mix of shows — light and serious, traditional and daring.

2 *Evening Joe* 6:15 p.m.

Join pre-theater crowds at **Joe Allen's** (326 West 46th Street; 212-581-6464; joeallenrestaurant.com; $$). It's a very busy, very New York place. While you're eating your meatloaf or pan-roasted Atlantic cod, check out the wall displays of posters for the biggest flops in Broadway history. You no doubt know the book, and the movie, of *Breakfast at Tiffany's*. But did you know there was also a 1966 musical version? It starred Mary Tyler Moore and

Richard Chamberlain. The world may have forgotten, but the stars no doubt haven't.

3 *Song and Dance* 7:45 p.m.

Get your theater weekend off to a high-energy start with a musical. Broadway is most famous for its musicals, and the top 14 longest running shows in Broadway history (No. 1 is *The Phantom of the Opera*) are creatures of song and dance. A tip: musicals that have been playing for years can sometimes be tired, with sets shopworn and stars long gone. Choose one that's still fresh, and arrive early. Latecomers are despised almost as much as people who forget to turn off their cellphones.

4 *Fisticuffs Optional* 10:30 p.m.

Head off for a drink at **Angus McIndoe** (258 West 44th Street; 212-221-9222; angusmcindoe.com), where producers, critics, stagehands, directors, and sometimes even actors show up to discuss what's playing, what's in rehearsal, and what's in trouble. A notorious incident here: the director David Leveaux, angry with Michael Riedel of *The New York Post* for making snide comments about his show at the time, a 2004 revival of *Fiddler on the Roof*, pushed, or maybe it was punched, Riedel. It's unlikely there will be another boxing match, but you never know.

SATURDAY

5 *45 Seconds Away* Noon

The legendary **Cafe Edison** (Hotel Edison, 228 West 47th Street; 212-840-5000; edisonhotelnyc.com; $)

OPPOSITE Times Square is at the heart of Broadway and home to the TKTS booth for discounted theater tickets.

RIGHT A production of *The Book of Mormon*, one of Broadway's success stories, at the Eugene O'Neill Theater.

looks like a plain deli, but to Broadway it is something like what the Polo Lounge is to Hollywood. Producers, writers, even old-time comedians have been known to hang out here — yes, that could have been Jackie Mason you saw here once, telling a bad joke. Neil Simon wrote a play called *45 Seconds From Broadway* about the Cafe Edison, but the restaurant is better than the play. August Wilson used to sit for hours over coffee working on his dramas. And another kind of star — Joe DiMaggio — lived at the Edison when he was hitting the kind of home runs that aren't just a metaphor for success. The cafe is also known as the Polish Tea Room, but you can order much more than tea — from bagels and lox to potato pancakes and applesauce to pastrami on rye.

6 *Get Serious* 1:45 p.m.

You want to see at least one meaty serious play, the kind with a chance of showing up someday on college reading lists. Schedule it for today's matinee, and you'll leave yourself time afterward to think about what you've seen and maybe even discuss it over dinner. While you're waiting for the show to begin, check out the "At This Theater" feature in your *Playbill* to see what giants of yesteryear appeared on the stage you'll be viewing. Humphrey Bogart became a star at the Broadhurst in 1935 in *The Petrified Forest*. Marlon Brando made his Broadway debut in 1944 in *I Remember Mama* at the Music Box (which was built by Irving Berlin) and astonished audiences as Stanley Kowalski in *A Streetcar Named Desire* in 1947 at the Ethel Barrymore.

7 *Dinner Break* 6:15 p.m.

Rebuild your strength with a French-inspired dinner at **Chez Josephine** (414 West 42nd Street, 212-594-1925; chezjosephine.com; $$$). It's run by Jean-Claude Baker, the adopted son of the chanteuse Josephine Baker. There's a pianist accompanying the meal — and whoever's playing that evening counts among his predecessors Harry Connick Jr. If you'd rather go Japanese, try **Kodama Sushi** (301

West 45th Street; 212-582-8065; $$), a home away from home for chorus lines, supporting casts, stage managers, and other theatrical types. Stephen Sondheim and William Finn have been spotted at the sushi bar, and the autographed posters on the wall from recent hits (and misses) add to the ambience. It's a neighborhood place, but the neighborhood is Broadway.

8 *Seeing Stars* 7:45 p.m.

For the biggest night of the week, find a show with top-tier leads. Then file in with the rest of what's likely to be a full audience, and share the night with the other star watchers. Seeking autographs? Head for the stage door right after the curtain drops, and don't be dismayed if you're part of a crowd. Celebrity actors are usually willing to pause before entering their limos and sign all of the *Playbill* copies thrust at them. Before the show, check out the theater itself: many Broadway houses are stars in their own right. Notice the ornate decoration, and remember the history. **The Lyceum** on West 45th Street, for example, dates to 1903 and was put up by a producer named David Frohman. The story has it that he built

ABOVE A cluster of theater marquees along West 45th Street between Eighth Avenue and Broadway.

BELOW Breakfast at Cafe Edison on West 47th Street, a regular gathering spot for Broadway royalty.

OPPOSITE Queuing for theater tickets at the TKTS booth in Time Square.

an apartment high up inside with a small door for observing the stage—and that he would wave a white handkerchief to warn his actress wife, Margaret Illington, that she was overacting.

9 *And More Stars* 11 p.m.

The post-performance star gazing is usually good at **Bar Centrale** (324 West 46th Street, 212-581-3130), where actors often retire for a cocktail after two or three hours of performing. It's run by Joe Allen, above his eponymous restaurant. Don't seek autographs here, though—the performers expect post-play privacy.

SUNDAY

10 *Brunch, Anyone?* 12:30 p.m.

If the weather's good, the idyllic garden of **Barbetta** (321 West 46th Street; 212-246-9171;

barbettarestaurant.com; $$$), is an enchanting space for a light pasta and a lighter wine, giving you a feel of northern Italy.

11 *Grand Finale* 2:45 p.m.

Make your last play memorable. Broadway and its audiences have fallen under the spell of Hollywood-style special effects, and if you want something splashy, you can probably find it. In theater, you're seeing the pyrotechnics live (despite all the publicity, accidents are rare), and producers can't rely as much on computer-generated sleight of hand. Sit back and enjoy the spectacle.

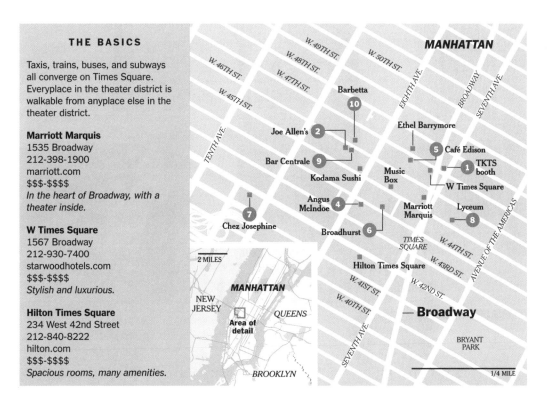

THE BASICS

Taxis, trains, buses, and subways all converge on Times Square. Everyplace in the theater district is walkable from anyplace else in the theater district.

Marriott Marquis
1535 Broadway
212-398-1900
marriott.com
$$$-$$$$
In the heart of Broadway, with a theater inside.

W Times Square
1567 Broadway
212-930-7400
starwoodhotels.com
$$$-$$$$
Stylish and luxurious.

Hilton Times Square
234 West 42nd Street
212-840-8222
hilton.com
$$$-$$$$
Spacious rooms, many amenities.

Harlem

In Harlem, the first decade of the 21st century may best be remembered for a seismic demographic shift: an influx of whites and a drop in the black population that put it below 50 percent for the first time in decades. This shifting landscape has brought with it a new cultural scene with a distinct cosmopolitan vibe. But even with the arrival of new doorman buildings, luxurious brownstone renovations, and chichi boutiques and restaurants, this swath of Upper Manhattan still brims with the cultural landmarks that made it the capital of black America. — BY JOHN ELIGON

FRIDAY

1 *The Collector* 4 p.m.

Stop in at the **Schomburg Center for Research in Black Culture** (515 Malcolm X Boulevard; 212-491-2200; nypl.org/locations/schomburg), a trove of manu-scripts, rare books, photos, videos, and recordings. Its exhibitions have included photos of early-20th-century Harlem life, private papers of Maya Angelou, and an exploration of the influence of jazz on the visual arts. It is named for Arturo A. Schomburg, a visionary Puerto Rican-born black private collector who amassed a significant portion of this material before his death in 1938. Check the schedule for films, lectures, discussions, and musical performances.

2 *Strivers' Row* 6 p.m.

The timing may not have been great when a group of elegant townhouses went up in Central Harlem in the late 19th century — it was shortly before an economic panic. But the development, on 138th and 139th Streets between Adam Clayton Powell Jr. and Frederick Douglass Boulevards, survived. Today it is one of New York's most graceful and integrated examples of period architecture. Stroll past Italian-palazzo and neo-Georgian former homes of the high achievers like Scott Joplin and Bill Robinson (Bojangles) who gave this section its nickname, **Strivers' Row**. Don't miss a nod to the

OPPOSITE Italianate and neo-Georgian townhouses line Harlem's Strivers' Row, once home of Scott Joplin.

RIGHT Named for one of New York's first black-owned bars, 67 Orange Street is on Frederick Douglass Boulevard.

past, painted on some of the entrances to the rear courtyard: "Private Road; Walk Your Horses."

3 *Culinary Eclectic* 8 p.m.

Marcus Samuelsson, true to his heritage as Ethiopian born and Swedish raised, has done with his restaurant, **Red Rooster Harlem** (310 Lenox Avenue; 212-792-9001; redroosterharlem.com; $$), what few can: attracted a clientele diverse in both color and age. The menu pulls from all cultural corners (blackened catfish, lemon chicken with couscous, steak frites with truffle Béarnaise). Stick around after dinner for a drink at the horseshoe-shaped bar or in the basement lounge.

4 *Old-world charm* 11 p.m.

After eating at Red Rooster, head downstairs to Samuelsson's other creation, **Ginny's Supper Club**. Although both are housed in the same building, Ginny's has its own unique speakeasy vibe and a different menu of creative small plates and cock-tails. With a DJ spinning tunes, you can dance off your dinner.

SATURDAY

5 *The Main Drag* 10 a.m.

The 125th Street corridor stands at the conver-gence of old and new. On the sidewalks, vendors sell fragrant oils and bootleg DVDs. Indoors, you can find shops like **La Scala NYC** (254 West 125th Street; 212-678-7889), an outlet for Ferragamo, Prada, and Dolce & Gabbana, and **S&D Underground** (136 West 125th Street; 212-222-1577), which stocks favorite urban brands. In the midst of it all is the **Apollo**

Theater (253 West 125th Street; 212-531-5300; apollotheater.org), where black entertainers have gotten their start for generations. Group tours are available by appointment; if you're not traveling with a pack, you may be able to tag along with one. (Call to check availability.) To catch the famed Amateur Night, return on a Wednesday.

6 *El Barrio* Noon

Harlem's east side is El Barrio, a repository for Spanish culture. Have an authentic Puerto Rican meal at **La Fonda Boricua** (169 East 106th Street; 212-410-7292; fondaboricua.com; $$), which started as a lunch counter and expanded with a simple dining room. There is no printed menu, but you can't go wrong with the pernil (roast pork). Walk off lunch with a tour of the murals on nearby buildings. A mosaic at 106th Street and Lexington Avenue honors Julia de Burgos, a 20th-century poet. The four-story-tall *Spirit of East Harlem*, on Lexington at 104th Street, includes men playing dominoes, a woman holding a baby, and the Puerto Rican flag. Stop at **Justo Botanica** (134 East 104th Street; 212-534-9140), a musty store founded in 1930 that offers spiritual readings and sells African and Native American carvings as well as prayer cards, candles, and beads. For a history of Spanish Harlem, visit **El Museo del Barrio** (1230 Fifth Avenue; 212-831-7272; elmuseo.org).

7 *The New Renaissance* 3 p.m.

The true Harlem Renaissance was centered on art, and now new galleries and art spaces are popping up again. **Casa Frela Gallery** (47 West 119th Street; 212-722-8577; casafrela.com), in a Stanford White brownstone, exhibits small collections and screens films. The **Renaissance Fine Art Gallery** (2075 Adam Clayton Powell Jr. Boulevard; 212-866-1660; therfagallery.com) and the **Dwyer Cultural Center** (258 St. Nicholas Avenue; 212-222-3060; dwyercc. org) celebrate black culture through art. **The Studio Museum** (144 West 125th Street; 212-864-4500; studiomuseum.org) shows fine art, photography, and film.

8 *The Scene* 6 p.m.

Hard to believe, but the stretch of Frederick Douglass Boulevard where the 1970s drug lord Frank Lucas boasted he made $1 million a day selling heroin is now Harlem's Restaurant Row, a stretch of inviting restaurants and lounges. If the weather's nice, enjoy a drink in the neighborhood's best outdoor space at **Harlem Tavern** (No. 2135; 212-866-4500; harlemtavern.com). Find an ode to multiculturalism at **bier international** (No. 2099; 212-280-0944; bierinternational.com), a twist on the German beer garden. Check out **Moca Restaurant & Lounge** (No. 2210; 212-665-8081; mocalounge.com) for the latest in hip-hop tracks. At No. 2082 and

named for the address of one of New York's first black-owned bars, **67 Orange Street** serves up exotic cocktails and a speakeasy vibe.

9 *Soul Food* 8 p.m.

Those who know soul food know that it is best prepared at home. So it should come as no surprise that good soul food restaurants are difficult to find even in Harlem. **Sylvia's** (328 Lenox Avenue; 212-996-2669; sylviassoulfood.com) gets the most buzz, but it's more about the restaurant's history than the food. Better options are **Amy Ruth's** (113 West 116th Street; 212-280-8779; amyruthsharlem.com; $), where dishes are named for famous blacks, or **Miss**

Mamie's Spoonbread Too (366 West 110th Street; 212-865-6744; spoonbreadinc.com; $-$$) and its sister restaurant **Miss Maude's** (547 Lenox Avenue; 212-690-3100). Perhaps the best hidden secret in Harlem soul food — and music — is **American Legion Post 398** (248 West 132nd Street; 212-283-9701; $). Every other Saturday, and on some other nights, the post hosts a jazz jam session in the basement of the brownstone it calls home. There is no cover for this can't-miss live show, and the drinks are cheap, as are the favorites like fried chicken and meatloaf, served on Styrofoam plates.

10 *A World of Music* 11 p.m.

For a great combination of live music and dance space, take a seat at **Shrine** (2271 Adam Clayton Powell Jr. Boulevard; 212-690-7807; shrinenyc.com), a no-frills restaurant and bar where everyone feels like a local. This is a true melting pot of music. Jazz, reggae, hip-hop, pop, and more might be played by the live

OPPOSITE Manuel Vega's mosaic tribute to the poet Julia de Burgos at East 106th Street and Lexington Avenue.

ABOVE The Abyssinian Baptist Church, where the Sunday-morning service is as theatrical as a Broadway production.

LEFT Dr. Harold Cromer puts on a tap dance show at the Dwyer Cultural Center.

bands on a single night. And with lots of floor space to maneuver in, you'll be dancing until your feet are sore.

SUNDAY

11 *Gospel and Brunch* 11 a.m.
　Gospel churches are a staple of Harlem visits. A tourist favorite is **Abyssinian Baptist Church** (132 Odell Clark Place; 212-862-7474), a megachurch with a Broadway-like music production. For something

more serene, yet still inspiring, attend a service at **Mount Olivet Baptist Church** (201 Lenox Avenue; 212-864-1155). Afterward, have your Sunday brunch at **Kitchenette Uptown** (1272 Amsterdam Avenue; 212-531-7600; kitchenetterestaurant.com; $$). The restaurant is designed like a rural porch, providing a home-style feel with hearty dishes to match. Try the baked crème brulee French toast, turkey sausage, or one of the thick omelets.

ABOVE A Rafael Ferrer exhibit at El Museo del Barrio in Spanish Harlem.

OPPOSITE Interior of Mount Olivet Baptist Church, 201 Lenox Avenue, at 120th Street, formerly Temple Israel.

THE BASICS

Harlem spans a section of northern Manhattan roughly from 110th Street to 155th Street.

Get around on the subway, or hail taxicabs.

Aloft Harlem
2296 Frederick Douglass Boulevard
212-749-4000
alofthotels.com/harlem
$$
A bona fide luxury hotel to represent Harlem's changing face. High design in contemporary style.

The Harlem Flophouse
242 West 123rd Street
347-632-1960
harlemflophouse.com
$$
Charming four-room bed and break-fast in an 1890s brownstone.

Mount Morris House
12 Mount Morris Park
917-478-6214
mountmorrishouse.com
$$$
Four-room B&B in a restored mansion with elegantly carved woodwork.

Map labels

W. 125TH ST.
S&D Underground
Studio Museum
Apollo Theater
Aloft Harlem
Dwyer Cultural Center
5
La Scala NYC
The Harlem Flophouse
Renaissance Fine Art Gallery
Moca Restaurant & Lounge
Kitchenette Uptown
AMSTERDAM AVE.
BROADWAY
FREDERICK DOUGLASS BLVD.
MORNINGSIDE PARK
Harlem Tavern **8**
bier international
Miss Mamie's Spoonbread Too
67 Orange Street
CENTRAL PARK N.
MANHATTAN
El Museo del Barrio
CENTRAL PARK
Justo Botanica
E. 104TH ST.

Harlem
W. 145TH ST.
HARLEM RIVER DR.
Strivers' Row
2
W. 138TH ST.
W. 135TH ST.
Abyssinian Baptist Church **11**
Miss Maude's
Schomburg Center for Research in Black Culture **1**
Shrine **10**
American Legion Post
MALCOLM X BLVD. (LENOX AVE.)
ADAM CLAYTON POWELL JR. BLVD.
Sylvia's **9**
Ginny's Supper Club **4**
Mount Olivet Baptist Church
Red Rooster Harlem **3**
Amy Ruth's
MARCUS GARVEY PARK
Mount Morris House
Casa Frela Gallery **7**
W. 116TH ST.
FIFTH AVE.
MADISON AVE.
PARK AVE.
LEXINGTON AVE.
THIRD AVE.
SECOND AVE.
FIRST AVE.
East Harlem
E. 110TH ST.
La Fonda Boricua **6**
EAST RIVER DR.
BRONX
Harlem R.
E. 125TH ST.
East River

Brooklyn

The Brooklyn Cruise Terminal on the Buttermilk Channel has picturesque views even when the Queen Mary 2, *which docks there regularly, is at sea. There is verdant Governor's Island across the water and, behind it, the heaving, jagged rise of Manhattan. To the north are the great bridges of the East River. To the west, the Statue of Liberty. And to the east, beyond chain link and forbidding streets, there is Brooklyn itself, New York City's most populous borough, a destination in its own right.* — BY SAM SIFTON

FRIDAY

1 *Waterfront Stroll* 4 p.m.

The cobblestone streets under the Manhattan Bridge are home to small shops and shiny new condominium buildings, and to **Saint Ann's Warehouse** (38 Water Street, at Dock Street; 718-254-8779; stannswarehouse.org), a theater that has been a mainstay of the Brooklyn arts scene for more than three decades. Located across from Fulton Ferry State Park, it is an excellent destination after a walk along the **Promenade** in Brooklyn Heights (parallel to Columbia Heights, a grand old street of towering brownstones, running from Remsen to Orange Streets). Check ahead to see what's playing and then wander down to the box office to pick up your tickets.

2 *Walk in the Park* 5 p.m.

Alternatively, head inland, toward the leafy precincts of Fort Greene, for a show at the **Brooklyn Academy of Music** (bam.org) or the **Mark Morris Dance Group** (markmorrisdancegroup.org). Atlantic Avenue, which runs deep into the borough, will lead you most of the way, through a stretch of antiques shops and restaurants.

3 *Pretheater Dinner* 6:30 p.m.

Once you get strolling, it is difficult not to drift into other pretty residential neighborhoods: Cobble Hill and Carroll Gardens nearby and, slightly farther

OPPOSITE Brownstone-lined streets invite long strolls in Park Slope and Prospect Heights.

RIGHT Boutiques like the Brook Farm general store flourish in Brooklyn's Williamsburg and Greenpoint neighborhoods.

afield, Park Slope and Prospect Heights. There is excellent eating along the way. At the bottom of Court Street in Carroll Gardens: **Prime Meats** (465 Court Street at Luquer Street; 718-254-0327; frankspm.com), a chic Germanish steak and salad restaurant. A block or so farther south, on the corner of Huntington Street: **Buttermilk Channel** (524 Court Street; 718-852-8490; buttermilkchannelnyc.com), where you can get local cheeses and pastas and a superlative duck meatloaf. Ten minutes before the end of your meal, have the host call for a car, and go to the performance you've chosen.

4 *Drink after the Curtain* 10 p.m.

Fort Greene abounds in bars suitable for a late-evening drink. A cocktail at the minimalist and homey **No. 7** is no-risk (7 Greene Avenue at Fulton Street; 718-522-6370; no7restaurant.com). Those seeking rougher charms can venture to the **Alibi** (242 DeKalb Avenue between Clermont Avenue and Vanderbilt Avenue), where there are cheap drinks, a pool table, and a crowd that runs equal parts artist and laborer.

SATURDAY

5 *Breakfast Paradise* 9 a.m.

Tom's Restaurant in Prospect Heights (782 Washington Avenue at Sterling Place; 718-636-9738) has been a crowded, friendly mainstay of this neighborhood for decades, and is a winning place to begin a day in Kings County (that's Brooklyn, to you outsiders; each of New York City's five boroughs

is a separate county). Eat pancakes and waffles in a room filled with tchotchkes and good cheer, and watch the marvelous parade.

6 *Parks and Arts* 10 a.m.

A Tom's breakfast provides a strong foundation for a visit to the exhibitions of the nearby **Brooklyn Museum** (200 Eastern Parkway at Washington Avenue; 718-638-5000; brooklynmuseum.org). It is also useful in advance of a walk through the **Brooklyn Botanic Garden** (900 Washington Avenue; 718-623-7200; bbg.org), a 19th-century ash dump that is now home to some of the best horticultural displays in the world. And of course there is **Prospect**

Park (prospectpark.org), Frederick Law Olmsted and Calvert Vaux's triumphant 1867 follow-up to Central Park in Manhattan. Those with children may wish to visit the zoo (450 Flatbush Avenue near Empire Boulevard; 718-399-7339; prospectparkzoo. com), where the daily feedings of the sea lions are a popular attraction.

7 *A Visit to Hipchester* 2 p.m.

Boutiques, coffee bars, and restaurants continue to flourish in Williamsburg and Greenpoint, north Brooklyn's youth-culture Marrakesh. Amid these, **Brook Farm**, a general store in south Williamsburg, offers an aesthetic of farmhouse cosmopolitanism (75 South Sixth Street, between Berry Street and Wythe Avenue; 718-388-8642; brookfarmgeneralstore.com). **Artists and Fleas** is a weekend market where artists, designers, collectors, and craftspeople showcase their work (70 North Seventh Street between Wythe Avenue and Kent Avenue; artistsandfleas.com).

ABOVE A storefront on Eighth Avenue in Brooklyn's Chinatown, in Sunset Park.

LEFT The much loved and well used Prospect Park, designed by Frederick Law Olmsted and Calvert Vaux after they completed Central Park in Manhattan.

OPPOSITE Diners in the back room of Williamsburg's Fatty 'Cue, the Southeast Asian inspired barbecue restaurant.

And **Spoonbill and Sugartown, Booksellers** offers an eclectic mix of art and design books and academic tracts (218 Bedford Avenue at North Fifth Street; 718-387-7322; spoonbillbooks.com). For a pick-me-up or a new coffee machine for home, try **Blue Bottle Coffee** (160 Berry Street between North Fourth and North Fifth Streets; 718-387-4160; bluebottlecoffee. net), an impossibly nerdy outpost of the original Oakland coffee bar. Siphon? French press? Cold drip? All available, along with all the crazy coffee talk you like. Get your geek on.

8 *Dinner for Kings* 7:30 p.m.

Those enamored of the Williamsburg scene may stay in the neighborhood for a smoky dinner at **Fatty 'Cue**, Zak Pelaccio's antic and awesome Southeast Asian barbecue joint (91 South Sixth Street between Berry Street and Bedford Avenue; 718-599-3090; fattycue.com). In Greenpoint, there is the excellent and slightly more adult-themed **Anella**, where the chef Joseph Ogrodnek works marvels with vegetables and duck (222 Franklin Street at Green Street; 718-389-8100; anellabrooklyn.com). Parents with children might try the pizzas at **Motorino** (319 Graham Avenue at Devoe Street; 718-599-8899; motorinopizza.com) or scoot back to Park Slope, where the brothers Bromberg offer a welcoming family atmosphere with food to match at their **Blue Ribbon Brooklyn** (280 Fifth Avenue, between

First Street and Garfield Street; 718-840-0404; blueribbonrestaurants.com).

9 *Pazz and Jop* 10 p.m.

Brooklyn's music scene continues to expand. Three places to hear bands are **Union Pool** in Williamsburg (484 Union Avenue at Meeker Avenue; 718-609-0484; unionpool.blogspot.com); **Brooklyn Bowl**, also there (61 Wythe Avenue between North 11th and North 12th Streets; 718-963-3369; brooklynbowl.com); and **Southpaw**, in Park Slope, (125 Fifth Avenue, between Sterling Place and St. Johns Place; 718-230-0236; spsounds.com). Jazz heads should make their way to **Barbès** in Park Slope (376 Ninth Street at Sixth Avenue; 347-422-0248; barbesbrooklyn.com), where a rich calendar of readings and concerts can take a visitor from early Saturday evening well into Sunday morning.

SUNDAY

10 *Dim Sum à Go-Go* 10 a.m.

Brooklyn's Chinatown, along Eighth Avenue in the Sunset Park neighborhood, is not as large as Manhattan's. But it offers great pleasures. Arrive early for a dim sum meal at **Pacificana** (813 55th Street at Eighth Avenue; 718-871-2880), and watch as the dining room fills into an approximation of a rush-hour subway car. Then stop in at **Ba Xuyen** (4222

Eighth Avenue, between 42nd and 43rd Streets) for a banh mi brunch sandwich and a Vietnamese coffee, or at the tiny **Yun Nan Flavour Snack** (775A 49th Street at Eighth Avenue) for a fiery sweet and sour soup with dumplings.

11 *History in the Ground* 1 p.m.
Walk off all the food with a tour of **Green-Wood Cemetery** (500 25th Street at Fifth Avenue; 718-768-7300; green-wood.com), the hilly and beautiful

parkland where generations of New Yorkers have moved after death. Admission is free, as are the maps available at the entrance. Look for Boss Tweed, for Jean-Michel Basquiat, for Leonard Bernstein and other once-boldfaced names, as parrots (really!) fly about and the wind ruffles the trees and that view of Manhattan opens up in the distance once more. It appears smaller from this vantage, as if placed in perspective.

ABOVE The view of Manhattan from the Battle Hill Monument at Green-Wood Cemetery, which was a popular tourist attraction in the 19th century.

OPPOSITE The pedestrian path on the Brooklyn Bridge.

THE BASICS

Take a taxi from LaGuardia or Kennedy Airport. From Kennedy, the AirTrain to Jamaica Station is also an option. From Manhattan, take the subway. Use the subway, buses, and car services, which are easier to find than yellow cabs.

Marriott at the Brooklyn Bridge
333 Adams Street
718-246-7000
marriott.com
$$$
Comfortable rooms and easy access to bus and subway.

Hotel Le Jolie
235 Meeker Avenue
718-625-2100
hotellejolie.com
$$
Boutique hotel in Williamsburg, near shops and restaurants.

Hotel LeBleu
370 Fourth Avenue
718-625-1500
hotellebleu.com
$$$
Sublime views of the harbor and near two subway stations.

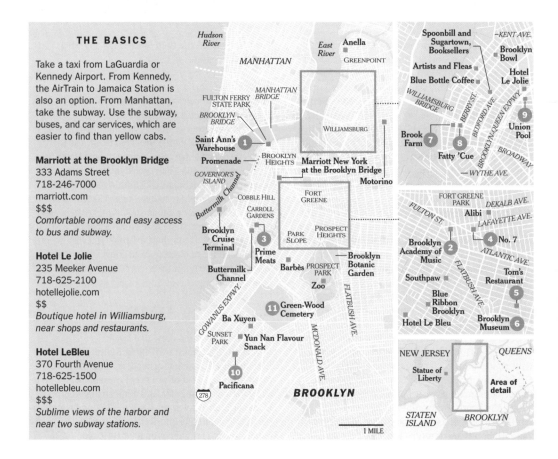

East Hampton

On the east end of Long Island, N.Y., the Atlantic Ocean crashes to the shores of the lavish string of villages known as the Hamptons. When New York City's movers and shakers migrate here in the summer for sunning, surfing, fishing, and flirting, the center of the social swirl is historic East Hampton. Lately a raft of luxurious boutiques and restaurants have opened in town. Beloved old hotels and barrooms have been renovated. And celebrities — including Madonna — keep snapping up property in the area.

— BY STEPHANIE ROSENBLOOM

FRIDAY

1 *Social Calendar* 4 p.m.

Want to plunge into the Hamptons social scene? Then your first order of business is to grab the free newspapers and glossy magazines — *Social Life, Hampton Life, Hamptons, Hampton Sheet, Dan's Papers, The East Hampton Star* — and scan them for the weekend's fete, charity event, or oceanfront screening of *Jaws*. You'll find them near the door of many boutiques in East Hampton, but perhaps the most indulgent place to get them is **Scoop du Jour** (35 Newtown Lane; 631-329-4883), the ice cream parlor where waffle cones are stacked with cavity-friendly flavors like cake batter and cotton candy. This is also where you can buy Dreesen's doughnuts, a Hamptons staple since the 1950s. Need a gift for a party host (or yourself)? Shops have sprouted along Main Street, including **Hugo Boss** (No. 46) and **Roberta Freymann** (No. 21).

2 *Pizza Patio* 7 p.m.

It's not just socialites who flee New York for the Hamptons in summer. Manhattan restaurateurs migrate here, too. Among the latest establishments is the Italian standby **Serafina** (104 North Main Street; 631-267-3500; serafinarestaurant.com: $$$). Yellow

umbrellas poke up like daffodils from its sidewalk patio and vine-covered pergola. Fresh pastas and seafood are on the menu, though the brick oven pizzas — in more than two dozen varieties, including pesto — are among the most popular picks. On a typical night, couples canoodle at the bar while well-manicured families stream into the dining room. If your taste leans toward fried seafood, home-made chowder, and frosty drinks, however, head to **Bostwick's Chowder House** (277 Pantigo Road; 631-324-1111; bostwickschowderhouse.com; $$), which has new indoor-outdoor digs.

3 *Water Music* 9 p.m.

Watching boats glide along the horizon is perhaps the simplest and most peaceful of Hamptons pleasures. Happily, a favorite haunt, the **Boathouse** (39 Gann Road; 631-329-3663; easthamptonboathouse.com), has expanded and relocated to a secluded spot overlooking Three Mile Harbor, where Bostwick's was previously located. The open-air decks of this gleaming restaurant are an idyllic perch from which to watch boats dock. But on weekends, as the night progresses, the Boathouse morphs into an indoor-outdoor lounge where the lithe and tanned sip and sway to beats from a D.J.

SATURDAY

4 *Farm Fresh* 10 a.m.

Before men in golf shirts roamed the Hamptons, it was the purview of farmers. Thankfully, there are

OPPOSITE At the Pollock-Krasner House and Study Center visitors don slippers to walk on the paint-splattered floor of Jackson Pollock's studio.

RIGHT A converted storage barn, which Jackson Pollock and Lee Krasner used as their studio, is open to tours at the Pollock-Krasner House and Study Center.

still some left. Pick up fresh eggs, local produce, and home-baked muffins and scones for breakfast at **Round Swamp Farm** (184 Three Mile Harbor Road; 631-324-4438; roundswampfarm.com). Be sure to buy enough for lunch so you can skip the interminable snack bar line at the beach.

5 *Where to Tan* 11 a.m.

Choosing a favorite Hamptons beach is not unlike choosing a favorite child. Still, two beaches were among the U.S. top 10 named in 2010 by Stephen P. Leatherman, director of the Laboratory for Coastal Research at Florida International University. **Coopers Beach** (in Southampton) captured the No. 1 spot, beating out beaches in Florida and California. And **Main Beach** (in East Hampton) took fifth place. Both are wide and clean and — very important — sell food. Many beaches require seasonal parking permits, though visitors can park at Coopers Beach for $40 a day. Parking at Main Beach is $20 a day, but weekdays only; on weekends visitors must walk or ride bikes. (For details, go to the Long Island Convention & Visitors Bureau's Web site, discoverlongisland.com.)

ABOVE East Hampton's Main Beach.

RIGHT Diners in the Boathouse, in a secluded spot overlooking Three Mile Harbor.

6 *East End Expressionism* 3:30 p.m.

The wetlands and dunes that draw pleasure-seekers today also inspired some of the greatest abstract and landscape artists of our time. Go see why at **LongHouse Reserve** (133 Hands Creek Road; 631-329-3568; longhouse.org), a sprawling but less-visited garden and sculpture park with works by Buckminster Fuller, Dale Chihuly, Willem de Kooning, and Yoko Ono. Founded by the textile designer Jack Lenor Larsen (who still lives there, according to docents), the reserve's nearly 16 acres are open to the public Wednesdays through Saturdays during the summer. Nearby is the **Pollock-Krasner House and Study Center** (830 Springs-Fireplace Road; 631-324-4929; pkhouse.org),

which Jackson Pollock and Lee Krasner bought for $5,000 in 1946 and turned into their home and studio. Visitors must don padded slippers to enter the barn because the floor is splattered with paint that Pollock dripped and flung for his masterpieces. In fact, some of his paint cans are still there.

7 *Clams and Cocktails* 8 p.m.

Norman Jaffe, the American architect, designed the once popular (and now shuttered) restaurant known as Laundry. The space has a new life as **Race Lane** (31 Race Lane; 631-324-5022; racelanerestaurant.com; $$$) — a sleek yet cozy spot with a tree-shaded patio seemingly engineered for tête-à-têtes over breezy cocktails and clams from the raw bar. Inside, well-heeled couples dine at tables or on couches in the spare, airy space. You'll find seafood dishes like red snapper with saffron and spinach, baked salmon with a ginger glaze over shiitake mushrooms and snow peas, or lobster salad with avocado.

8 *No Velvet Rope* 10 p.m.

The Hamptons nightclub scene has quieted in recent years as action shifts to the tip of Long Island at Montauk, where shabby motels and quaint restaurants are being remade into boho chic establishments. But there are still plenty of pleasures to be had in East Hampton after sunset.

The music continues to thump at clubs like Lily Pond and, now, RdV East. Another hot spot is the newly renovated **c/o The Maidstone** (207 Main Street; 631-324-5006; themaidstone.com). The hotel's Living Room restaurant and lounge lure a lively, attractive crowd.

SUNDAY

9 *Morning Runway* 11:30 a.m.

Catch a tennis match or baseball game on flat screens while enjoying panini or frittatas at **CittaNuova** (29 Newtown Lane; 631-324-6300; cittanuova.com; $$$), a Milan-inspired cafe with a facade that peels back to provide indoor-outdoor seating along the village's prime shopping strip. A backyard patio has more tables. The pretty space can be jammed during events like the World Cup. Should there be no games to hold your attention, people-watching (O.K., fashion-policing) from the outdoor tables will.

10 *Artful Afternoon* 1 p.m.

Many of the artists who settled in the Hamptons exhibited at **Guild Hall** (158 Main Street; 631-324-0806;

ABOVE The upscale boutique of New York designer Roberta Freymann.

guildhall.org), the region's celebrated arts center, and current artists still do. Performances are held all summer long.

11 *Behind the Hedges* 2:30 p.m.
Real estate is a blood sport here. And one of the most coveted addresses is Lily Pond Lane. Take a leisurely drive along the wide road where beyond the hedges you can glimpse houses that belong to the likes of Martha Stewart. Grey Gardens,

once the decayed home of Edith Ewing Bouvier Beale and her daughter, can be found where Lily Pond meets West End Road. Along the way you're likely to spot many material girls, but if you are desperately seeking the original, head over to Bridgehampton, where Madonna owns a horse farm on Mitchell Lane.

ABOVE Sampling the merchandise at Scoop du Jour. Ice cream is part of a Hamptons weekend, along with beaches, seafood, and mingling with Manhattan socialites.

OPPOSITE Everybody into the water at Main Beach. Popular pastimes on the sandy beaches of the Hamptons include sunning, surfing, fishing, and flirting.

THE BASICS

The drive from Manhattan can be lengthy in heavy summer traffic. Try the Long Island Railroad, Hampton Jitney (hamptonjitney.com), or even the Hampton Luxury Liner (hamptonluxuryliner.com). Rent a bicycle once you're there.

c/o The Maidstone
207 Main Street
631-324-5006
themaidstone.com
$$$$
19 modish rooms, beach parking permits, vintage Scandinavian bicycles, and yoga classes.

The 1770 House Restaurant & Inn
143 Main Street
631-324-1770
1770house.com
$$$$
Feels like the home it once was.

The Huntting Inn
94 Main Street
631-324-0410
thepalm.com/Huntting-Inn
$$$-$$$$
A pretty inn that is also home to the popular Palm restaurant.

Map labels:

4 MILES

Gardiners Bay · Block Island Sound

SHELTER I. · Boathouse ③ · Pollock-Krasner House and Study Center · Montauk

SPRINGS FIREPLACE RD. · Napeague Bay

Little Peconic Bay

SUFFOLK · **East Hampton**

Bridgehampton

OSBORNE LN. · Serafina ②

East Hampton

LONG ISLAND R.R. · N. MAIN ST.

CittaNuova

NEWTOWN LN. · ⑨ · Roberta Freymann

Southampton · Atlantic Ocean

⑤ Coopers Beach

① · Scoop du Jour · MAIN ST. · Hugo Boss

— OLD NORTHWEST RD. · THREE MILE HARBOR RD. ④

—HANDS CREEK RD.

Longhouse Reserve ⑥ · Round Swamp Farm · SUFFOLK

114 · East Hampton Train Station · **Area of detail** · LONG ISLAND R.R. · 27 Amagansett · Bostwick's Chowder House

Race Lane ⑦ · PANTIGO RD.

East Hampton

1770 House Restaurant & Inn · Huntting Inn

MONTAUK HWY · 27 · ⑧ · c/o The Maidstone · ⑩ Guild Hall

LILY POND LN. · Atlantic Ocean

Grey Gardens ⑪ · Main Beach

— WEST END RD. · 1 MILE

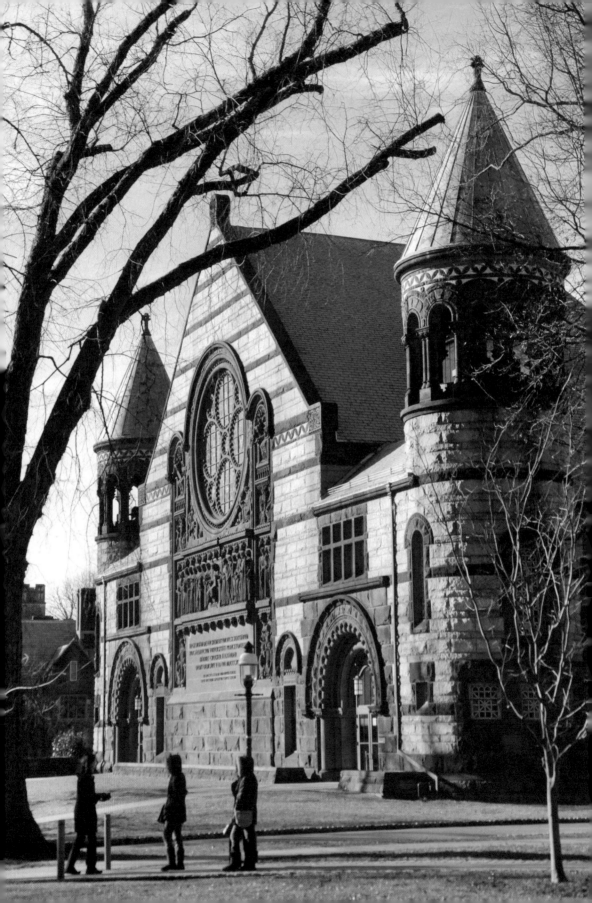

Princeton

"I think of Princeton as being lazy and good-looking and aristocratic — you know, like a spring day," F. Scott Fitzgerald wrote in This Side of Paradise. *Ninety years later, the appraisal still fits. From the century-old wrought-iron FitzRandolph Gate of Princeton University to the sleek rowing shells on sparkling Lake Carnegie, this small New Jersey town retains an air of easygoing noblesse. It is studded with landmarks, from a Revolutionary War battlefield to Albert Einstein's workplace, but nevertheless lives firmly in the present — traditional but not stuffy, charming but not quaint. In the tree-shaded downtown, Colonial-era buildings and high-end spots coexist with jeans-and-corduroy vegetarian hangouts and ice cream shops. And the campus is its own luxurious green city, in the words of Raymond Rhinehart, author of a guide to campus architecture, "a marketplace of ideas, set in a garden."* — BY LOUISE TUTELIAN

FRIDAY

1 *Catch of the Day* 6 p.m.

There's great fishing at the **Blue Point Grill** (258 Nassau Street; 609-921-1211; bluepointgrill.com; $$-$$$). The menu typically lists 20 fish specials, from Barnegat bluefish to a whole Greek bronzini. It's B.Y.O., but not to worry: **Nassau Liquors Grape & Grain** (264 Nassau Street; 609-924-0031) is a handy half-block away.

2 *The Flavor of the Place* 8 p.m.

Get out onto Nassau Street, Princeton's main street, to window-shop the bookstores and boutiques, check out vintage buildings, and peek down side streets at beautifully kept Victorian houses. The red-brick **Bainbridge House** (158 Nassau Street), dating to 1766, is now the Historical Society of Princeton. The Tudor Revival building at 92 Nassau Street, built in 1896, was once a Princeton dormitory.

SATURDAY

3 *Stack 'em Up* 8 a.m.

Get up and go early to **Pj's Pancake House** (154 Nassau Street; 609-924-1353; pancakes.com; $$), Princeton's breakfast nook since 1962, with the initial-carved wooden tables to prove it. Students, young families, and gray-haired couples rub elbows while plunging their forks into the tender pancakes — buttermilk, blueberry, buckwheat, and more — served with eggs and bacon. Afterward, stroll down to the **Princeton University Store** (114 Nassau Street; 609-921-8500) and pick up a map of the university campus. (Online maps are at princeton.edu.)

4 *Take a Tiger by the Tail* 9 a.m.

The bronze tigers flanking the entrance to Nassau Hall are a fitting invitation to the architecturally rich Princeton University campus, though their dignity is compromised by the generations of children who have clambered over them. Built in 1756, Nassau Hall survived bombardment in the Revolution and now holds the office of the university president. Alexander Hall has echoed with the words of speakers from William Jennings Bryan to Art Buchwald; Prospect House, deeper into the campus, was Woodrow Wilson's home when he was president of the university. Don't be surprised if a wedding is under way at University Chapel, a Gothic-style landmark. The Frank Gehry-designed Peter B. Lewis math and science library, opened in 2008, adds swooping stainless steel curves to Princeton. The 87,000-square-foot building includes a second-floor "tree house" with 34-foot-high ceilings and clerestory windows framing the trees outside. All over campus,

OPPOSITE Alexander Hall has echoed with the words of speakers from William Jennings Bryan to Art Buchwald.

BELOW The 18th-century Nassau Inn.

look for unusual spires and whimsical gargoyles of cackling monkeys, dinosaurs, and dragons.

5 *Art in the Heart of Campus* 10:30 a.m.

Besides giving Princeton one of the richest endowments of any university in the world, wealthy benefactors have provided it with a wealth of outstanding art at its **Art Museum** (609-258-3788; artmuseum.princeton.edu). Don't rush it — there are more than 60,000 works, and the galleries are spacious, peaceful, blessedly uncrowded — and free. The pre-Columbian and Asian collections are notable, but you can also see Monet's *Water Lilies and Japanese Bridge* and Warhol's *Blue Marilyn*. If you remember reading the 2004 best-selling novel *The Rule of Four*, set on the Princeton campus, picture the student heroes sneaking around these premises in the dark.

6 *Follow the Icons* 12:30 p.m.

Pick up a sandwich on excellent fresh bread at **Witherspoon Bread Company** (74 Witherspoon Street; 609-688-0188; terramomo.com; $) and set out to trace the footsteps of giants. "It's a fine fox hunt, boys!" George Washington is said to have cried to his troops as the British fled from them on Jan. 3, 1777, at **Princeton Battlefield** (500 Mercer Road in neighboring Princetown Township; 609-921-0074; state.nj.us/dep/ parksandforests/parks/princeton.html). The victory

helped restore faith in the American cause. Check the small museum and picture the troops clashing where students now sunbathe. Back toward town on Mercer Road, turn right onto Olden Lane to reach the **Institute for Advanced Study** (Einstein Drive; 609-734-8000; ias.edu). Einstein used to walk to work there from his house at 112 Mercer Street — sometimes, legend has it, after forgetting to put on his socks. The buildings, still a rarefied haven for distinguished scholars, are closed to the public, but the 500-acre Institute Woods, where violets bloom along the banks of the Stony Brook, is open to the public year-round.

7 *Relativity and Retail* 3 p.m.

Only in Princeton will you find a store that combines an Einstein mini-museum with great deals on woolens. Walk directly to the rear of **Landau of Princeton** (102 Nassau Street; 609-924-3494; landauprinceton.com) to see the Einstein photos, letters, and sketches. Then check out the pop-top mittens made of Alpaca yarn, perfect for texting. Steps away in Palmer Square, dozens of shops sell well-designed and indulgent goods from eye kohls to stemware and sandals. Revive at **The Bent Spoon** ice cream shop (35 Palmer Square West; 609-924-2368; thebentspoon.net), whose owners pledge to use local, organic, and hormone-free ingredients whenever possible in the treats they make fresh every day. Who knew nectarine sorbet could taste so good?

8 *For the Record* 5 p.m.

Since 1980, the **Princeton Record Exchange** (20 South Tulane Street; 609-921-0881; prex.com) has been dispensing used vinyl, CDs, and DVDs at irresistible prices (from $2 for some LPs to under $12 for used DVDs). The store, which is open until 9 p.m., crams 150,000 items onto its floor at any one time.

9 *Sustainable Dining* 8 p.m.

One relaxing choice for dinner is **Mediterra** (29 Hulfish Street; 609-252-9680; terramomo.com; $$$), where wines from 10 countries line the walls; look for paella or locally raised chicken. Locally sourced and sustainable food is the focus at **elements** (163 Bayard Lane; 609-924-0078; elementsprinceton.com; $$$). Golden tilefish, black bass and monkfish are all from area waters.

10 *Brews and Blues* 10 p.m.

You may hear anything from pop to blues to classic rock 'n' roll for a modest cover at **Triumph Brewing Company** (138 Nassau Street; 609-924-7855; triumphbrewing.com), where the crowd is student-heavy but not raucous. A busy bar dispenses hand-crafted beers, and graduate students rub elbows with 40-somethings escaping their teenage children.

SUNDAY

11 *The Tow Path* 11 a.m.

Rent a mountain bike at **Jay's Cycles** (249 Nassau Street, 609-924-7233; jayscycles.com) and cruise southeast on Alexander Street for about a mile and a half until you see Turning Basin Park on the right. You'll be next to the Delaware-Raritan Canal tow path, a level dirt trail that is a delightful place to walk, bike, or jog. If you'd rather be on the

water, you can stow the bike at **Princeton Canoe & Kayak Rental** (483 Alexander Street; 609-452-2403; canoenj.com) and rent a watercraft. Make your way a half-mile up to the Washington Road Bridge and look for impossibly fit young Princetonians sculling under a bright blue spring sky on Lake Carnegie.

ABOVE Regulars can browse the 150,000 or so titles at the Princeton Record Exchange, open since 1980. The store is known for its selection of vinyl.

OPPOSITE Students walk the Princeton University campus, which in the words of Raymond Rhinehart is "a marketplace of ideas, set in a garden."

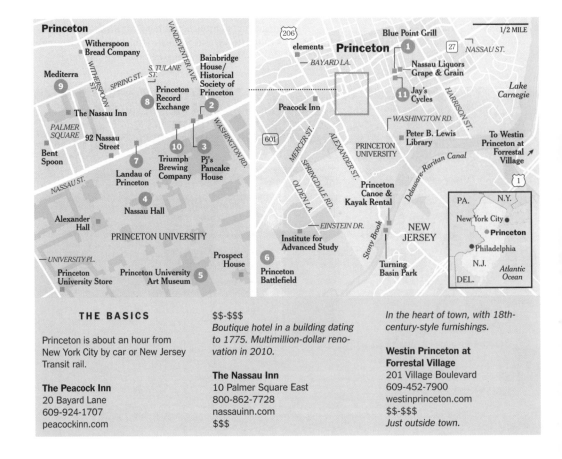

THE BASICS

Princeton is about an hour from New York City by car or New Jersey Transit rail.

The Peacock Inn
20 Bayard Lane
609-924-1707
peacockinn.com

$$-$$$
Boutique hotel in a building dating to 1775. Multimillion-dollar renovation in 2010.

The Nassau Inn
10 Palmer Square East
800-862-7728
nassauinn.com
$$$

In the heart of town, with 18th-century-style furnishings.

Westin Princeton at Forrestal Village
201 Village Boulevard
609-452-7900
westinprinceton.com
$$-$$$
Just outside town.

Cape May

Located at the very southern tip of New Jersey (Garden State Parkway Exit 0), Cape May combines an authentic Victorian past with the present-day ambience of a summer beach town. The entire city of about 3,700 is a National Historic Landmark, and for good reason: there are no fewer than 600 sturdily built Victorian homes and buildings on this 3.5-square mile island. Located on the Atlantic Flyway, Cape May is also an internationally renowned birding hot spot, and devotees cluster there in spring and fall when the birds stop over on their way to distant climes. In summer, another migration takes place, as suntanned masses who don't know a pigeon from a plover descend on this tony resort. — BY LOUISE TUTELIAN

FRIDAY

1 *Bird's Eye View* 4 p.m.

Get the lay of the land by climbing to the top of the **Cape May Lighthouse**, built in 1859 (Lighthouse Road, Cape May Point State Park; capemaymac.org; 800-275-4278). At the top, you'll be rewarded for your 199-step trek with a panoramic view of the Cape May Peninsula, and neighboring coastal locations from Wildwood, New Jersey, to the north to — on a clear day — Cape Henlopen, Delaware, to the west. The 157-foot-tall light also offers interpretive exhibits about its history and information on the lives of its former keepers.

2 *Back in Time* 7 p.m.

Tucked in a corner of Congress Hall (251 Beach Avenue; 609-884-8422; congresshall.com; $$), a restored 19th-century grand hotel, the **Blue Pig Tavern** is the place to refuel. Entrees range from its signature seafood pot pie with shrimp, scallops, and crab to four styles of burgers with house-cut fries and slaw. You will be one of a long list of visitors to this space. It was the first tavern in Cape May, a gathering place for whalers in the 1700s.

OPPOSITE The Cape May Lighthouse, a favorite landmark of this traditional summer beach town.

RIGHT The wildlife refuge at Cape May Point is a rest stop on the migratory path along the Atlantic Seaboard for millions of birds. This guest is a cedar waxwing.

3 *Kick Back* 9 p.m.

Congress Hall doesn't dwell in the past, however. In its basement is the **Boiler Room Bar**, a nightclub with bare brick walls and 10 TV monitors so every guest gets a view of the acts that perform nearly every weekend. And yes, it really was the hotel's boiler room.

SATURDAY

4 *On the Wing* 8 a.m.

Cape May is on the Atlantic Flyway, one of the planet's busiest migratory corridors, navigated by hundreds of species in spring and fall. Because of its location amid barrier islands and wetlands, freshwater and ocean, birds come to rest, eat, and nest. Things are calmer in summer, but there are still plenty of birds to be seen, especially with the help of a good guide. The **Cape May Bird Observatory** (701 East Lake Drive, Cape May Point; 609-884-2736; birdcapemay.org) sponsors naturalist-led walks from 8 to 10 a.m. on Saturdays at Cape May Point State Park on Lighthouse Avenue. Participants can expect to see waterfowl, flycatchers, warblers, piping plovers, and more. The Observatory's Northwoods Center offers free maps for self-guided walks.

5 *Tour a Mansion* 11 a.m.

The **Emlen Physick Estate** (1048 Washington Street; 800-275-4278; capemaymac.org) is a mansion constructed for a Philadelphia physician in the Stick style of the late 1800s. If you are an architecture buff, or even if you're not, take the 45-minute guided tour. Fifteen of the rooms have been restored with historical accuracy, shedding light on how residents lived in the Victorian era, when so many of Cape May's majestic houses were built.

ABOVE Whalers were once regulars at the Blue Pig.

BELOW Cape May's beach, at the far southern tip of New Jersey, has attracted sun seekers since the Victorian era.

6 *Pick a Panini* 1 p.m.

Skip the Victorian tea sandwiches and head to **Tisha's** (322 Washington Street in the Washington Street Mall; 609-884-9119; tishasfinedining.com; $$) for more contemporary fare. Locals love the restaurant's sandwiches, paninis, and soups, as well as entrees like vegetable salad with grilled shrimp or a bacon bleu burger. The menu changes seasonally.

7 *Beach Bake* 2 p.m.

Hit the beach where the locals do, at the Cove. Located on Beach Avenue at 2nd Street, at the very beginning of the Promenade, **Cove Beach** has a lovely view out toward the Lighthouse at Cape May Point. It's an old-school, laid-back spot that's not overly groomed, making it ideal for beach-combing in search of Cape May's plentiful frosted, etched sea glass. From Memorial Day through Labor Day, you'll need a beach pass, available for a small fee at every beach entrance.

8 *Romantic Glow* 6 p.m.

Everyone looks spectacular in the golden light shed from the intricate chandeliers at the **Ebbitt Room**. Claim a lipstick-red banquette in this intimate space tucked off the lobby of the **Virginia Hotel** (25 Jackson Street; 800-732-4236; virginiahotel.com; $$$) and settle in. The menu changes often, but you might find items like fennel, apple, and celery root salad with blood orange vinaigrette; pomegranate braised short rib; and a decadent milk chocolate caramel tart for dessert.

9 *Curtain Up* 8 p.m.

How many shore towns can boast two professional theater companies? The **Cape May Stage** (Lafayette and Bank Streets; 609-884-1341; capemaystage.com) presents a full season in its 75-seat theater. Productions have included *Say Goodnight, Gracie* by Rupert Holmes, about the legendary George Burns; *The Understudy* by Pulitzer Prize nominee Theresa Rebeck, the-behind-the-scenes tale of a Broadway show; and *Steel Magnolias*, Robert Harling's tale of love among a band of close friends in the South. At the **East Lynne Theater Company** at First Presbyterian Church (500 Hughes Street; 609-884-5898; eastlynnetheater.org), recent fare has included *He and She* by Rachel Crothers and *The World of Dorothy Parker*, adapted by Gayle Stalhuth.

ABOVE Hundreds of Victorian houses and inns give Cape May its distinctive architectural look.

BELOW Birders do some flocking of their own each spring and fall at Cape May.

SUNDAY

10 *The Wheel Thing* 8 a.m.

The boardwalk closes to bicycles at 10 a.m. So get up early to ride its entire length. Many Cape May hotels provide bicycles for their guests — it's bike-friendly on these streets. You can also rent from the conveniently located **Shields Bike Rentals** (11 Gurney Street; 609-898-1818) or the **Village Bicycle Shop** (605 Lafayette Street; 609-884-8500).

11 *Munch Brunch* 10 a.m.

For Sunday brunch, the **Mad Batter** (19 Jackson Street; 609-884-5970; madbatter.com; $$) serves tempting dishes like Chesapeake Bay Benedict with lump crabmeat or orange and almond French toast. Indulge with a pomegranate mimosa — one of six varieties.

ABOVE It's 199 steps to the top (and 199 back down), but the panoramic view of New Jersey and Delaware from the Cape May Lighthouse is worth the climb.

OPPOSITE Elaborate gingerbread exteriors, a hallmark of lavishly decorated Victorian houses, survive in style in Cape May. This building is the Virginia Hotel.

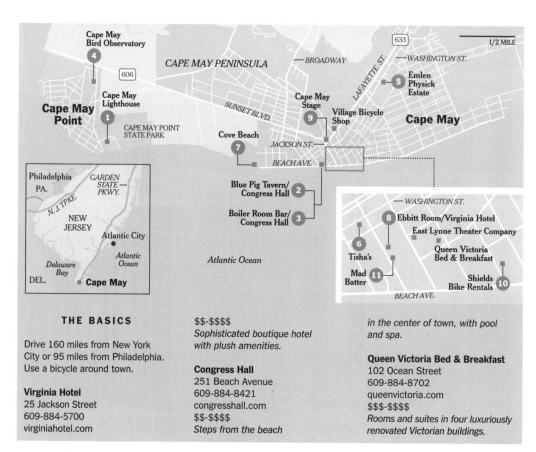

THE BASICS

Drive 160 miles from New York City or 95 miles from Philadelphia. Use a bicycle around town.

Virginia Hotel
25 Jackson Street
609-884-5700
virginiahotel.com

$$-$$$$
Sophisticated boutique hotel with plush amenities.

Congress Hall
251 Beach Avenue
609-884-8421
congresshall.com
$$-$$$$
Steps from the beach

in the center of town, with pool and spa.

Queen Victoria Bed & Breakfast
102 Ocean Street
609-884-8702
queenvictoria.com
$$$-$$$$
Rooms and suites in four luxuriously renovated Victorian buildings.

Philadelphia

The 18th-century city tucked inside Philadelphia, where the United States was born at Independence Hall, swarms all year with curious tourists, history buffs, and children on school trips. Sprawling out from it is the other Philadelphia, firmly rooted in the 21st century and bustling with the activity of a rapidly evolving destination city. Adventurous restaurants reinforce the city's growing culinary reputation, though an obligatory cheese steak still hits the spot. Neighborhoods in transition provide hot spots for shopping and night life, while other areas keep dishing out some old-school Philly "attytood." And traditional leisure-time stops like the Schuylkill riverbanks and the venerable Franklin Institute keep right on drawing them in.
— BY JEFF SCHLEGEL

FRIDAY

1 *Another Go-to Building* 3:30 p.m.

Independence Hall belongs to the ages; **City Hall** (Broad and Market Streets; 215-686-2840; visitphilly.com/history/philadelphia/city-hall) belongs to Philadelphia. This 548-foot-tall 19th-century building is more than just a big hunk of granite interrupting traffic in the heart of the city — it is topped by a 27-ton bronze statue of William Penn, one of 250 statues by Alexander Milne Calder ornamenting the building inside and out. Take the elevator to the top ($5) for 35-mile views from the observation deck.

2 *No Lemon Meringue Pie* 5:30 p.m.

Silk City Diner Bar & Lounge (435 Spring Garden Street; 215-592-8838; silkcityphilly.com) is a twofer with a lower-level nightclub on one side and a traditional diner car on the other with atmospheric, dim red lighting. Grab a counter seat at the diner and choose from a copious selection of bottled beer or a cocktail like the Pink Panther strawberry martini.

OPPOSITE AND RIGHT Philadelphia's massive City Hall is topped by a bronze statue of William Penn weighing 27 tons. Artist Alexander Milne Calder was responsible for the structure's 250-plus statues, including this likeness of Benjamin Franklin (right).

3 *Odd Couple* 7 p.m.

The Chinese-Peruvian fusion at **Chifa** (707 Chestnut Street; 215-925-5555; chifarestaurant.com; $) can kill two cravings with one dish. Chef and owner Jose Garces's fourth Latin-flavored restaurant in town spotlights chifa, a cuisine influenced by Peru's 19th-century Chinese immigrants. Meals start with a bowl of yuca-flour bread balls, a warm, doughy treat dipped in tangy whipped guava butter. The small-plate menu is an amalgam of tastes — the chaufa blends stir-fried rice with a hint of spicy chorizo, topped with sweet soy-glazed scallops. Chupe is a succulent seafood chowder with mussels, shrimp, and purple potatoes.

4 *In a League of Its Own* 10 p.m.

The Big Lebowski meets sleek lounge at **North Bowl** (909 North Second Street; 215-238-2695; northbowlphilly.com), a converted mechanics' garage where segments of original concrete floor and brick wall blend with brightly painted walls, abstract art, and glow-in-the-dark bowling pins. There are 13 lanes of bowling on the first floor, four lanes on the second, and bars on both floors. The soundtrack one night included Blondie and Cuban rhythms; fish tacos and thai beef skewers were on the menu to cure a case of late-night munchies.

SATURDAY

5 *One Man's Labyrinth* 10 a.m.

Some places can't be fully captured by just photos and words. That sums up **Philadelphia's Magic Gardens** (1020-1022 South Street; 215-733-0390; philadelphiasmagicgardens.org), an art center and endearingly bizarre outdoor maze of mortar, bicycle tires, bottles, textiles, artwork, and tchotchkes. The Philadelphia mosaic muralist Isaiah Zagar's magnum opus is a multitextured, multilayered labyrinth that leaves visitors amused, if maybe puzzled. "I think it communicates something, but I don't know what that is," said Mr. Zagar, who frequently roams his creations and obligingly fields questions from visitors.

6 *Slice of Local Color* 11 a.m.

Enticing aromas of homemade sausages, cheeses, and pastries infuse the air along the **Ninth Street Italian Market** (Ninth Street, between Wharton and Fitzwater Streets; phillyitalianmarket.com). Produce vendors ply their wares under green-and-red awnings in front of shops selling Italian specialties and assorted merchandise at this century-old South Philadelphia outdoor market. Hungry? **Lorenzo's Pizza** (Ninth and Christian Streets; 215-922-2540; lorenzospizza.net) is an unpretentious corner shop serving one of the city's best pizza slices. The secret: they don't skimp on spices.

7 *Ben's Place* 1:30 p.m.

Noted for its giant two-story model of a human heart and interactive displays that make it seem more like a theme park than a science museum, the **Franklin Institute** (222 North 20th Street; 215-448-1200; fi.edu) is aptly named for Benjamin Franklin, the city's favorite polymath. Flight simulators, giant locomotives parked indoors, a virtual trip to astronaut world—it's tough to know where to look. The place to start, though, may be on the Web, where you can buy tickets in advance and skip the long lines waiting at the door.

8 *Sewing for Goths* 4 p.m.

Fabric Row (Fourth Street, between South and Catherine Streets) has long been the place to buy a bolt of cloth. Fabric shops still ply their trade there, but they share the street with tattoo parlors and an eclectic mix of retailers in this energetic Queen Village neighborhood. **Armed & Dangerous** (623-625 South Fourth Street; 215-922-4525) sells wares in the "romantic gothic vein," along with a variety of imported Venetian ball masks ($25 to $300). **Bus Stop** (750 South Fourth Street; 215-627-2357;

ABOVE A jogger strikes a *Rocky*-esque pose atop the stairs of the Philadelphia Museum of Art.

OPPOSITE Rowers make their way down the placid Schuylkill River.

busstopboutique.com) specializes in designer shoes from Europe and South America, including the French-designed, Spanish-made Coclico brand and the eco-friendly brand Terra Plana.

9 *Israeli and More* 8 p.m.

Housed in a blocky building in Society Hill and decked out in the dun colors of Jerusalem stone, **Zahav** (237 St. James Place; 215-625-8800; zahavrestaurant.com; $$$) features Israeli recipes and a healthy dose of North African and Middle Eastern fare, too. The ta'yim tasting menu is a good place to start for the uninitiated — first up is a bowl of creamy hummus and a large round of house-baked, earthy flat bread, followed by three small plates and then dessert. The Sabra is flavorful grilled chicken served over fluffy couscous; the salad is a potpourri of eight small dishes that include spicy Moroccan carrots seasoned in cumin and chilies that make your mouth zing.

10 *Down It if You Dare* 10 p.m.

If absinthe is your thing, head to the second-floor lounge at **Time** (1315 Sansom Street; 215-985-4800; timerestaurant.net). It dispenses five versions of the green liqueur, which until recently was banned in the United States. It was the drink of choice among 19th-century Parisian artists, not to mention Ernest Hemingway. If it's not your thing, the downstairs whiskey bar features around 75 scotches and other whiskeys. One late night in the dining room across the foyer, a freewheeling seven-piece jazz band played a raucous gig as some members took breaks in midtune to mingle with the crowd before jumping back in.

SUNDAY

11 *Morning Constitutional* 8:30 a.m.

The best time to hit **Independence National Historic Park** (nps.gov/inde) is first thing in the

morning, ahead of the crowds. Pick up your free tickets (the Visitor Center at 6th and Market Streets opens early) and start with the main attraction, Independence Hall, where lines will soon be longest. Take a quick look at the Liberty Bell through the glass at its dedicated building, and then poke around the restored buildings and inviting lawns.

12 *Riverside* 11 a.m.

Head over to the **Philadelphia Museum of Art** (26th Street and Benjamin Franklin Parkway; 215-763-8100; philamuseum.org), take your picture

with the Rocky statue out front, and then walk in to enjoy the collection. From there, walk behind the museum to the **Breakaway Bikes** shed (215-568-6002; breakawaybikes.com) to rent a bike ($10 an hour, helmet and lock included), and ride along the path paralleling the Schuylkill River in Fairmount Park. Look for elegant Victorian-era boathouses built in the heyday of the city's rowing clubs. One of the city's Olympic-level rowers was Grace Kelly's father. Watch today's rowers in their shells as they glide along the river, and take a look at some of the park's sculptures.

ABOVE AND OPPOSITE Philadelphia views from City Hall's observation deck. Above, the downtown skyline, and opposite, the grand Benjamin Franklin Parkway, which cuts through Logan Circle before terminating at the Philadelphia Museum of Art.

THE BASICS

Fly, drive, or take a train on Amtrak's busy Northeast Corridor. Philadelphia is a good walking city, but a car is handy.

The Independent
1234 Locust Street
215-772-1440
theindependenthotel.com
$$
Boutique hotel in a restored building. Some of the 24 rooms have fireplaces.

The Alexander Inn
301 South 12th Street
215-923-3535
alexanderinn.com
$$
Art Deco-inspired touches in 48 designer rooms.

Hotel Palomar
117 South 17th Street
215-563-5006
hotelpalomar-philadelphia.com
$$
Stylish new hotel near City Hall, with 230 rooms.

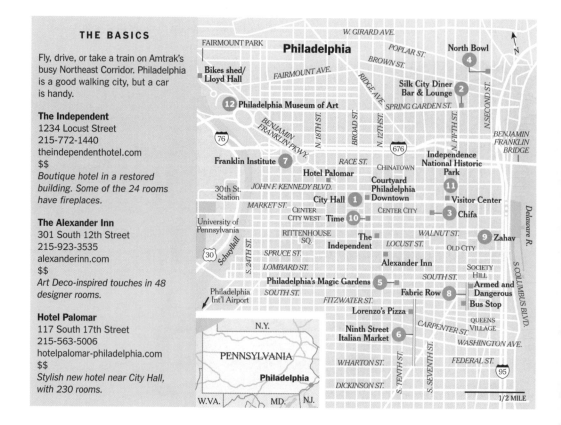

The Brandywine Valley

Only 15 miles from downtown Wilmington, Delaware, the Brandywine Valley is worlds away from the high-rise towers of the city center. Nestled into the northwest corner of Delaware and the southeast section of Pennsylvania, Brandywine, with its historic stone houses and rolling hills, would still look familiar to George Washington, who commanded the Continental Army there in 1777. Later, titans of industry, most notably the du Pont family, built lavish estates that are now open to the public. And artists like Andrew Wyeth made the landscape famous. But the Brandywine Valley is perhaps best enjoyed on horseback or by canoe, following the lazy path of the river, with a picnic and a good bottle of wine from one of the many local vineyards. — BY ANN COLIN HERBST

FRIDAY

1 *Happy Trails* 3:30 p.m.

Brandywine is horse country, but even if you have no equestrian skills, you can still get into the local spirit on an evening trail ride at **Gateway Stables** (949 Merrybell Lane, Kennett Square, Pennsylvania; 610-444-1255; gatewaystables.com). Meander the trails past 200-year-old oaks and enjoy the spectacular scenery of Gateway's 80 wooded acres and meadows skirting the Delaware border. Hourlong excursions for one to four riders are about $40 a person. Helmets are provided; sturdy shoes are recommended. Reservations are required.

2 *Tavern Dining* 5 p.m.

Imbibe some local color at **Buckley's Tavern & Restaurant** in Centreville, Delaware (5812 Kennett Pike/Route 52; 302-656-9776; buckleystavern.org; $$). The building dates to 1817; in the 1930s, the house became a tavern. Choose a pub favorite like fish and chips or look for dinner fare like roasted herb chicken or blackened tuna.

3 *Flowers and Fountains* 7 p.m.

Take advantage of long summer hours to take in the eye-popping horticultural displays at **Longwood Gardens**, Pierre du Pont's former country estate (Route 1, Kennett Square; 610-388-1000; longwoodgardens.org). Longwood's history dates to 1700, when the Peirce family bought the property

from William Penn. In 1906, du Pont bought the land and designed formal rose, wisteria, peony, and conservatory gardens. Italian-style water gardens, topiaries, and a series of fountains light up at night, with music. Admission is $18.

SATURDAY

4 *Wyeths and More* 9:30 a.m.

Housed in a 19th-century grist mill, the **Brandywine River Museum** contains a collection of American illustrations, still lifes, landscapes, and the artwork of three generations of the Wyeth family (Route 1, Chadds Ford, Pennsylvania; 610-388-2700; brandywinemuseum.org). The museum offers vistas of the Brandywine River. Highlights include the original oils by N.C. Wyeth (1882-1945) that were used to illustrate classics like *Treasure Island* and *Robin Hood*. In the Andrew Wyeth Gallery, you may see some of the Helga paintings and works focusing on local subjects like the Kuerner Farm. Also in the museum are works by Albert Bierstadt, Jasper Cropsey, and Asher Durand, as well as a collection of paintings by Jamie Wyeth.

OPPOSITE A Gilbert Stuart portrait of George Washington decorates the dining room of Winterthur, Henry Francis du Pont's country estate.

BELOW A garden picnic at the Chaddsford Winery.

5 *Gather at the River* Noon

You can't visit the Brandywine Valley without spending some time on the Brandywine River. **Wilderness Canoe Trips** (2111 Concord Pike/Route 202, Wilmington; 302-654-2227; wildernesscanoetrips.com) will provide the equipment, and a van puts you in on the Pennsylvania side and picks you up downstream two hours later in Delaware. But don't worry; the river does most of the work, leaving you free to enjoy the view of Brandywine Creek State Park in Delaware, where you might see deer, blue herons, turtles, carp, and bass. Rentals are about $55 for a canoe or tandem kayak, $45 for a one-person kayak. Before heading to the river, pick up a picnic at **Spring Run Natural Foods** (909 East Baltimore Pike, Kennett Square; 610-388-0500; springrunfoods.com), where you can forage an organic, nitrite-free feast.

6 *A Landmark Collection* 4 p.m.

This is du Pont country, and another of the family's contributions is **Winterthur** (5105 Kennett Pike/Route 52, Wilmington, Delaware; 302-888-4600; winterthur.org), Henry Francis du Pont's mansion of 175 rooms decorated in period American furnishings from 1640 to 1860. There are some 85,000 objects, from Chippendale furniture to paintings by Gilbert Stuart, John Singleton Copley, and Charles Willson Peale. The Chinese export porcelain includes 66 pieces from a dinner service once owned by George Washington. The nearly 1,000-acre property has acres of gardens that demonstrate du Pont's naturalistic principles of garden design and can be toured by tram.

7 *Mushrooms and Microbrews* 8 p.m.

Kennett Square bills itself as the Mushroom Capital of the World, and indeed, mushrooms have been a thriving local industry since the late 19th century. Start your evening at the **Half Moon Restaurant & Saloon** (108 West State Street, Kennett Square; 610-444-7232; halfmoonrestaurant.com; $$) with a plate of Chester County exotic mushrooms served with cranberries and walnuts on ciabatta

bread with melted Gorgonzola. If the evening is mild, try one of the bottled Belgian beers in the rooftop garden. (Downstairs at the bar, beers are on tap.) For dinner, you may want to have your mushrooms with an exotic meat like wild boar or kangaroo. For dessert, head to **La Michoacana Homemade Ice Cream** (231 East State Street, Kennett Square; 610-444-2996) for authentic Mexican ice cream, sorbet, and fruit bars in flavors like corn and rice pudding.

SUNDAY

8 *Wyeths' World* 9 a.m.

Members of Brandywine's most famous artistic family have been known to turn up for breakfast at **Hank's Place**, a wood-paneled diner that is a low-key local favorite (at the southwest intersection of Routes 1 and 100, Chadds Ford; 610-388-7061; hanks-place.net; $). Specialty egg dishes are served daily.

9 *An Infamous Day* 10:30 a.m.

Sept. 11, 1777, was a bad day on the Brandywine for George Washington. His troops tried and

ABOVE Mounting for a trail ride from Gateway Stables.

BELOW The conservatory at Longwood Gardens, one of the du Pont family estates in the area that are open to the public for tours.

failed to stop the advancing British, who went on to take Philadelphia. The **Brandywine Battlefield Park** (1491 Baltimore Pike/Route 1, Chadds Ford; 610-459-3342; brandywinebattlefield.org) recalls the story at a visitors' center with a small, low-tech collection of Colonial cannons, sabers, and other artifacts, including Continental currency. Also at the site are the headquarters of Washington and the Marquis de Lafayette, who was only 19 years old when he was wounded at Brandywine.

10 *Out of the Cellar* 1 p.m.
Sniff and sample at **Chaddsford Winery** (632 Baltimore Pike/Route 1, Chadds Ford; 610-388-6221; chaddsford.com), founded in 1982 and based in a

handsome 18th-century barn. The owners offer daily tastings of their wines—pinot noir, chardonnay, merlot, and more. Tour the winemaking and barrel-aging cellars, and for a bit of the Brandywine Valley to savor later, buy a bottle to take home.

ABOVE Buckley's Tavern is in a building dating back to 1817, but the restaurant's menu breaks from traditional fare. If the weather's nice, the front porch and back patio offer outdoor seating; if it's chilly, sit inside by the fire.

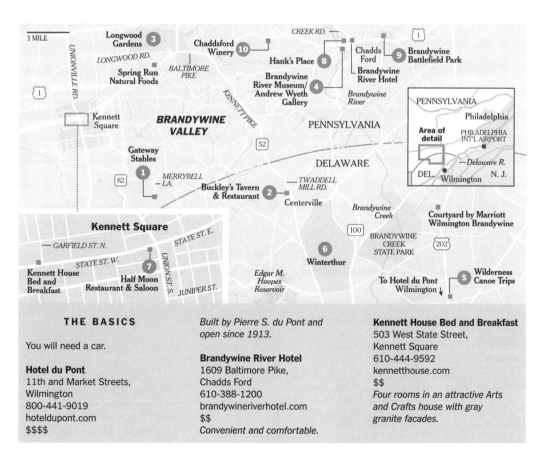

THE BASICS

You will need a car.

Hotel du Pont
11th and Market Streets,
Wilmington
800-441-9019
hoteldupont.com
$$$$

Built by Pierre S. du Pont and open since 1913.

Brandywine River Hotel
1609 Baltimore Pike,
Chadds Ford
610-388-1200
brandywineriverhotel.com
$$
Convenient and comfortable.

Kennett House Bed and Breakfast
503 West State Street,
Kennett Square
610-444-9592
kennetthouse.com
$$
Four rooms in an attractive Arts and Crafts house with gray granite facades.

New London

Ships have been sailing into the deep harbor of New London, Connecticut, since 1646 — schooners and packet ships, an English armada led by Benedict Arnold, nuclear submarines that glide silently up the Thames River, cresting the water like whales. The town helped shape Eugene O'Neill, who set two of his greatest plays at his family's New London cottage, and as tall ships visit and ferries disgorge cars and passengers from Long Island and Block Island, its salty flavor still feels real. New London's struggles are real, too, evidenced by some empty storefronts. But with huge pots of flowers bedecking lampposts and luxury apartments renting in once-neglected buildings, a new liveliness blends with breathtaking harbor vistas, glimpses of history, and the enduring draw of the sea. — BY MAURA J. CASEY

FRIDAY

1 *Lobster in the Rough* 7 p.m.

A little difficult to find, but worth the persistence, is **Captain Scott's Lobster Dock** (80 Hamilton Street; 860-439-1741; captscotts.com; $), a warm-months-only lobster shack with seating at outdoor picnic tables. It's off Howard Street, nestled between railroad tracks and a sheltered marina. The right choice here is the lobster roll, served cold or hot with drawn butter drizzled over generous chunks of lobster. Order the red potatoes, too, and if you're still hungry, have some ice cream.

2 *Rock around the Clock* 8 p.m.

New London's music scene has become more varied and vibrant in the last several years, with downtown bars hosting bands several nights a week for cover charges under $10. **The Oasis Pub** (16 Bank Street; 860-447-3929; oasisnewlondon.blogspot.com) is the spirited — some would say raucous — center of the local indie rock scene and sometimes hosts touring acts. The **El 'n' Gee Club** (86 Golden Street; myspace.com/thegee860) showcases punk, rock, and metal bands. The Bank Street Café (639 Bank Street; 860-444-1444; bankstreetcafe.com) features original

OPPOSITE Halfway between New York City and Boston, New London is an old New England port town that not only looks the part but still plays it, welcoming craft from pleasure boats to submarines in its deep-water harbor.

music and spotlights blues and country. About a mile or so from downtown is **Stash's Cafe** (95 Pequot Avenue; 860-443-1095; stashs.com), home to alternative rock bands.

SATURDAY

3 *Breakfast with Cannons* 9 a.m.

Sniff the flowers as you order sticky buns, scones, and your caffeine of choice at the **Thames River Greenery/Beanery** (70 State Street; 860-443-6817), a combination flower shop and coffee bar. You won't lack for reading material, either, as the shop opens out into City News, a store that offers more than 100 journals, magazines, and newspapers for sale. Pause at an outside table to watch for ships cruising down below past the Union Railroad Station, which was designed by H. H. Richardson, and listen for Amtrak trains whistling their way through it. Then take your repast to **Fort Trumbull State Park** (90 Walbach Street; 860-444-7591), a massive 19th-century fortification with jaw-dropping views of the Thames (New World pronunciation: Thaymes) and Long Island Sound. There are few prettier places for a picnic and few more pleasant ways to get a sense of New London's history and strategic location than by strolling around the fort, now a state park, inspecting the cannons and ramparts.

4 *Gallery Stroll* 11 a.m.

Small, distinctive galleries dot the downtown area, all within an easy walk. Stop in at **Yah-Ta-Hey Gallery** (279 State Street; 860-443-3204; yahtaheygallery.com) to see Native American art. **Hygienic Art** (81 Bank Street; 860-447-3240; hygienic.ning.com) is a residential art cooperative with rotating exhibits. **The Gallery at Firehouse Square** (239 Bank Street; 860-443-0344; firehousesquare.com) specializes in nautical art.

5 *Choose Your Asia* 1 p.m.

In the time-honored tradition of seaports everywhere, New London attracts a population from far-flung parts of the world, and on State Street, you can choose an inexpensive lunch from several national cuisines. **Bangkok City** and **Little Tokyo** (860-442-6970 and 860-447-2388) serve Thai and Japanese cuisine under the same roof at 123 and 131 State Street. Steps

away, **Northern Indian Restaurant** (150 State Street; 860-437-3978) offers a generous lunch buffet for about $10.

6 *Ah, Dramatists* 2 p.m.

When Eugene O'Neill wrote his detailed set directions for *Long Day's Journey Into Night* and *Ah, Wilderness!* he was recreating the living room and surroundings of **Monte Cristo Cottage** (325 Pequot Avenue; 860-443-5378 extension 285; theoneill.org/ prog/monte/montprog.htm), the summer home his family owned from 1884 to 1921, down to the wicker chairs and the wood of the writing desk. This cottage, where the O'Neills loved, suffered, and laughed as the characters do in these autobiographical plays, looks much as it did onstage. Tours run regularly from Memorial Day through Labor Day and by appointment the rest of the year with the exception of O'Neill's birthday, October 16, when the house is usually open for readings from his plays.

7 *A Drink with Eugene* 5 p.m.

O'Neill played on the New London waterfront as a boy and drank there as an adult. To follow in his footsteps, first look over the bronze statue at the foot of State Street based on a picture of him at age 7 sitting on the banks of the Thames River, and then take a seat at the **Dutch Tavern** (23 Green Street; 860-442-3453), legendary as the only remaining New London watering hole that he frequented. The owners are proud that the place, with its tin ceiling and century-old tables, still looks largely as it did in O'Neill's day. This is a basic bar, small and no-frills, but it serves a variety of ales and nonalcoholic drinks. It has been the setting for readings of O'Neill plays, among them, appropriately, *The Iceman Cometh*.

ABOVE Fort Trumbull, forbidding from the water but, once on the grounds, a great place to picnic.

RIGHT The young Eugene O'Neill, in bronze, at the waterfront where he played as a boy.

8 *Pasta and Malbec* 7 p.m.

Relax over dinner at **Tony D's** (92 Huntington Street; 860-443-9900; tonydsrestaurant.com; $$), a family-run New London favorite. Don't expect surprises here, but do count on reliable renditions of the standards, from homemade ravioli to eggplant parmigiana and veal piccata. For dessert, you will of course order cannoli.

9 *Jazz It Up* 8 p.m.

New London music isn't all indie and rock. Several times a month, celebrated and emerging jazz artists like Cyrus Chestnut, Tierney Sutton, and Sophie Milman play at the intimate 120-seat Oasis Room in the **Garde Arts Center**, (325 State Street; 860-444-7373; gardearts.org). And you'll never know what will be playing in the center's 1,450-seat restored vaudeville palace, the **Garde Theater** (built in 1926). On any given week it may be hosting contemporary music, touring Broadway musicals, symphony orchestras, opera, or dance. Its giant movie screen shows contemporary, international, and classic films.

SUNDAY

10 *Wake Up on the Boardwalk* 10 a.m.

A great place for a morning walk or a brisk swim is **Ocean Beach Park** (off Ocean Avenue), established after homes in the area were wiped out by the Great Hurricane of 1938. The park has a wide, sandy beach with a half-mile-long boardwalk, a water slide,

several restaurants, an Olympic-size swimming pool, and, on clear days, sparkling views of Long Island and Fishers Island, New York. When you've worked up an appetite, move on to **Muddy Waters** (42 Bank Street; 860-444-2232; $) for bagels, yogurt, muffins, or a breakfast sandwich with egg, tomato, baby spinach, cheese, and bacon. Don't forget a mug of Mystic Roasters coffee, espresso, or cappuccino.

11 *Shipping News* 1 p.m.

The **Custom House and Maritime Society Museum** (150 Bank Street; 860-447-2501; nlmaritimesociety.org) operates in a building that is also the oldest operating customs house in the United States. An 1833 jewel by Robert Mills, the designer of the Washington Monument, it has vaulted ceilings and a flying staircase. Two doors are made of wood taken from Old Ironsides, the storied battleship *Constitution*. (When the ship, commissioned in 1797, was being refurbished in the 1830s, some of its original wood was offered for public buildings.) The exhibits include ships' logs from the 1700s and artifacts from the whaling industry that was New London's economic base in the early 1800s. The permanent exhibit "*Amistad*: A True Story of Freedom" tells the story of the escaped slaves who commandeered the schooner *Amistad* in 1839.

ABOVE Its maritime history makes New London a stop for sailing ships like this replica of Henry Hudson's *Half Moon*.

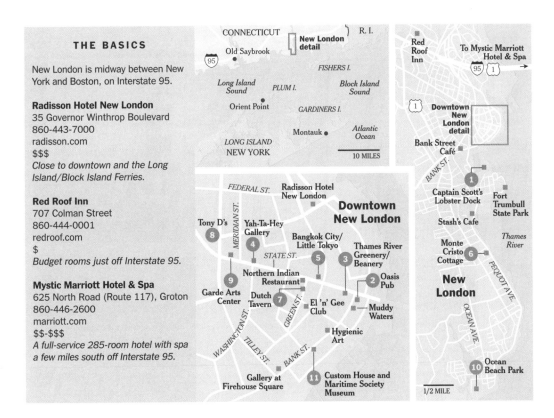

THE BASICS

New London is midway between New York and Boston, on Interstate 95.

Radisson Hotel New London
35 Governor Winthrop Boulevard
860-443-7000
radisson.com
$$$
Close to downtown and the Long Island/Block Island Ferries.

Red Roof Inn
707 Colman Street
860-444-0001
redroof.com
$
Budget rooms just off Interstate 95.

Mystic Marriott Hotel & Spa
625 North Road (Route 117), Groton
860-446-2600
marriott.com
$$-$$$
A full-service 285-room hotel with spa a few miles south off Interstate 95.

CONNECTICUT
New London detail
Old Saybrook
R. I.
95
FISHERS I.
Long Island Sound
PLUM I.
Block Island Sound
Orient Point
GARDINERS I.
Montauk
Atlantic Ocean
LONG ISLAND
NEW YORK
10 MILES

Red Roof Inn
To Mystic Marriott Hotel & Spa
95 1

1 Downtown New London detail

Bank Street Café

BANK ST.

Captain Scott's Lobster Dock
Fort Trumbull State Park

Stash's Cafe

Monte Cristo Cottage
Thames River

New London

PEQUOT AVE.

OCEAN AVE.

10 Ocean Beach Park

1/2 MILE

FEDERAL ST.
Radisson Hotel New London
MERIDIAN ST.
Tony D's
8
Yah-Ta-Hey Gallery
4
Bangkok City/Little Tokyo
STATE ST.
5
3
Thames River Greenery/Beanery
Northern Indian Restaurant
2 Oasis Pub
9
Garde Arts Center
Dutch Tavern
7
GREEN ST.
El 'n' Gee Club
Muddy Waters
WASHINGTON ST.
TILLEY ST.
BANK ST.
Hygienic Art
Gallery at Firehouse Square
11 Custom House and Maritime Society Museum

Downtown New London

New London

Providence

In its early days, Rhode Island was known as "Rogues' Island," a reference to the willingness of its founder, Roger Williams, to accept every element of society, as well as (more memorably) every religion—a distinct departure from the usual 17th-century custom. A few centuries later, Providence is still a hodgepodge, and a charming one. The revitalized waterfront and gleaming new downtown, including the Dunkin' Donuts Convention Center, complement colonial brick buildings and tidy frame houses spruced up in one of the country's most successful preservation efforts. Ivy League college students, a cutting-edge art school, and top-flight chefs all help define a newly energized city. But Providence still remembers, too, how to feel like a small town. — BY KAREN DEUTSCH

FRIDAY

1 *Espresso in the Air* 5 p.m.

Federal Hill (providencefederalhill.com) offers a different kind of Providence history and vibe, one that owes more to food than to colonial iconoclasts. Stroll down Atwells Avenue, center of the city's Little Italy, where the scent of sopressata drifts overhead. Much of the crowd checking out the food shops and boutiques is under 30, and the neighborhood is gentrifying, but there's still a small old-school contingent that congregates over pepper biscuits and pignoli. An espresso on **Caffe Dolce Vita's** outdoor patio (59 DePasquale Plaza; 401-331-8240; caffedolcevita.com) and a coin toss into the DePasquale Fountain will get you into the mood. This might also be the time to book a gondola ride (**La Gondola**; WaterPlace Park; 401-421-8877; gondolari.com) on the river for another day.

2 *Top Tomato* 8 p.m.

No one questions that **Al Forno** (577 South Main Street; 401-273-9760; alforno.com; $$$) put Providence on the culinary map three decades ago. And while some foodies prefer the town's splashier new kitchens, no one does rustic Italian better than Al Forno's

owners, George Germon and Johanne Killeen. Favorites include handmade bread gnocchi with spicy sausage, crackling grilled pizzas, and homemade ice cream. For those who like things intimate, Germon and Killeen also run a 20-seat Mediterranean tapas restaurant called **Tini** (200 Washington Street, 401-383-2400; thetini.com).

SATURDAY

3 *I'll Have Mine with Lemon* 9 a.m.

Walk under the playful pink-and-green lettering (easy to read isn't the point here) of the sign on **Brickway on Wickenden**'s facade (234 Wickenden Street; 401-751-2477; brickwayonwickenden.com; $) and take a table for coffee and a breakfast hearty enough to satisfy the hungry young Brown University students who might be at the next table. The menu offers the standards—bacon, eggs, omelets—plus some surprises, like the lemon blueberry French toast.

4 *Walking Back in Time* 10:30 a.m.

Stroll out and take a long look at some of the architecture that gives Providence its powerful sense of place. The **Rhode Island Historical Society** (401-331-8575; rihs.org) gives 90-minute walking tours of Benefit Street, a quaint strip that sits on College Hill, austerely overlooking modern condos. Find the former **State House** (150 Benefit Street; 401-222-3103) where, in 1776, Rhode Islanders declared independence two months before the rest of the American colonies. Wander through the **John Brown House Museum** (52 Power Street; 401-273-7507), completed

OPPOSITE A street in the College Hill neighborhood, home to Brown University and the Rhode Island School of Design.

RIGHT Gondola tours are a good fit in a city with three rivers and its own Little Italy.

in 1788 and home to one of the founders of Brown University. Another highlight is the **Providence Athenaeum** (251 Benefit Street; 401-421-6970; providenceathenaeum.org), founded in 1753.

5 *Across the Universe* 1 p.m.

Keep your walking shoes on and turn into the picturesque Brown campus (brown.edu), founded in 1764. Murmur sweet nothings at the rear archway to the **Metcalf Chemistry Building** (190 Thayer Street), a microcosmic whispering gallery for shy romantics. Enjoy the patriotic air at **University Hall** (1 Prospect

Street), where George Washington accepted an honorary degree in 1790. You can also contemplate the fate of H.P. Lovecraft (*Weird Tales, At the Mountains of Madness*), Providence's pulp fiction aficionado and author, who was denied entrance to Brown in the early 20th century after a nervous breakdown prevented his high school graduation.

6 *Shopping Street* 3 p.m.

Ready for a rest? Stop in at one of the cafes on Westminster Street, but don't linger too long. This is shopping country. Women congregate at shops like **Queen of Hearts** (No. 222; 401-421-1471; queenofheartsprovidence.com), which offers one-of-a-kind fashion choices, and the shoe emporium **Modern Love** (No. 220; 401-421-1476). The androgynous **Clover** boutique (No. 233; 401-490-4626; cloverprovidence.com) carries casual knits for her and button-downs for him.

7 *Diner Chic* 7:30 p.m.

Once upon a time, **Nicks on Broadway** (500 Broadway; 401-421-0286; nicksonbroadway.com;

ABOVE *WaterFire*, a river installation by the sculptor Barnaby Evans that comes to shimmering life downtown on Saturday nights from May to October.

LEFT Nicks on Broadway, a diner gone upscale.

$$-$$$) was a classic, hash-slinging diner. Then a local chef snapped up the diner and gave the blue-plate specials a culinary twist. The menu changes, but expect plenty of seafood, including the likes of oysters on the half-shell or pan-roasted striped bass.

8 *Watermark* 9:30 p.m.

In 1994, a Brown alumnus and artist named Barnaby Evans created a sculpture of 100 mini-bonfires that marked the convergence of the Providence, Moshassuck, and Woonasquatucket Rivers in the heart of downtown. The work, *WaterFire* (waterfire.org), continues today, drawing crowds on Saturday evenings between May and October.

9 *Tap Dance* 11 p.m.

Welcome the wee hours at **Local 121** (121 Washington Street; 401-274-2121; local121.com), a restaurant and nightspot in a hotel dating from the

1890s. Young crowds mix with old style as students and artists dance amid the stained-glass and Art Deco décor.

SUNDAY

10 *Graduate's Showing* 10 a.m.

The **RISD Museum** (224 Benefit Street; 401-454-6500; risdmuseum.org) of the Rhode Island School of Design houses 84,000 pieces, from ancient Greek statues to French Impressionist paintings and contemporary sculpture. The permanent collection includes attractive examples of the kind of furniture and interiors that once decorated Providence's colonial houses. But it's safe to expect something more daring as well. Past exhibitions have ranged from eccentric giant glass creations of Dale Chihuly, an RISD graduate, to a show of works made entirely of Styrofoam.

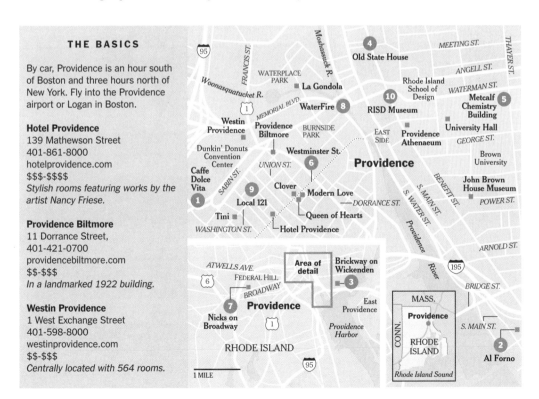

THE BASICS

By car, Providence is an hour south of Boston and three hours north of New York. Fly into the Providence airport or Logan in Boston.

Hotel Providence
139 Mathewson Street
401-861-8000
hotelprovidence.com
$$$-$$$$
Stylish rooms featuring works by the artist Nancy Friese.

Providence Biltmore
11 Dorrance Street,
401-421-0700
providencebiltmore.com
$$-$$$
In a landmarked 1922 building.

Westin Providence
1 West Exchange Street
401-598-8000
westinprovidence.com
$$-$$$
Centrally located with 564 rooms.

Newport

Each summer, two million tourists head to Narragansett Bay to shuffle their way through the Gilded Age trophy homes of Newport, Rhode Island — the lumbering white elephants (or are they overdressed maiden aunts?) perched hip to hip on the city's glittering rocky coastline. You too can explore America's insatiable appetite for… darn nearly everything here, and ponder the freakishness of the wealthy. Glut your senses by driving down Newport's main drag, otherwise known as Bellevue Avenue, a weird bazaar of architectural expression that includes more Versailles references than is probably healthy. If you continue along Ocean Drive, you will note attempts by contemporary architects to be this century's Stanford White (and that is not necessarily a good thing). But keep your eyes on the rugged coast, green parks, and yacht-filled harbor, all cooled on hot summer days by the ocean breeze, and you will remember how all of this got here.

— BY PENELOPE GREEN

FRIDAY

1 *The Cliff Walk* 3 p.m.

Get a jump on the weekend crowd with a Friday-afternoon trip to the Fifth Avenue of nature walks. Newport's famous **Cliff Walk** (cliffwalk.com) runs for three and a half miles along shoreline that makes everyone love an ocean view. It can be jam-packed on the weekends with tourists ogling the backyards of the Bellevue Avenue estates, many of which it slices into. Here is a strategy: Park at Easton's Beach on Memorial Boulevard, just below the Chanler at Cliff Walk hotel. You will find the path entrance right there. Follow the path to the end at Ledge Road (only if you are strong; this will take more than an hour) or to the stone staircase called the 40 Steps (about 20 minutes). Walk up Ledge Road to Bellevue Avenue, make a left, and you will see a bus stop for Newport's trolleys (if you make it only to the 40 Steps, there is a stop at Narragansett and Ochre Point). Take a trolley back

into town, get off at the Newport Casino, and walk down Memorial Boulevard to your car.

2 *Find Salvation* 7 p.m.

Have drinks and dinner at the **Salvation Restaurant and Bar** (140 Broadway; 401-847-2620; salvationcafe.com; $$), the way the locals do. The tattooed waiters and vaguely Asian-hippie menu remind you that Newport is only 40 miles from the Rhode Island School of Design. On the drinks menu, Tiger Tea is described as "an Arnold Palmer for the amoral set." Dinner can jump from a bamboo basket appetizer with vegetable dumplings and edamame to an entree of hanger steak. Stick around for dessert.

SATURDAY

3 *Eggs at the Dock* 9 a.m.

Take an outdoor table for breakfast at **Belle's Cafe**, at the Newport Shipyard (1 Washington Street; 401-846-6000; newportshipyard.com; $$). The eggy burritos are good, and the yacht-people watching is, too.

4 *A Heart-Shaped World* 10 a.m.

One of Stanford White's prettiest and silliest houses is **Rosecliff** (548 Bellevue Avenue), built for the heiress Tessie Oelrichs in 1902. You can read all about it in *The Architect of Desire*, a hypnotic family memoir about the tragic and emotional legacy of the Gilded Age's favorite architect, written by his great-granddaughter, Suzannah Lessard. (Tessie died alone at Rosecliff in 1926, Lessard wrote, talking to

OPPOSITE The Breakers, one of the trophy mansions that typified Newport's golden age and are now open for tour.

RIGHT The 3.5-mile Cliff Walk, where the public enjoys the Gilded Age plutocrats' treasured ocean views.

imaginary guests.) With its heart-shaped double staircase and baby-blue trompe-l'oeil ballroom ceiling, Rosecliff is sweeter and lighter than many of Newport's lavish hulks from the same period. Allow an hour for a tour of the house and a little more time to wander Rosecliff's green lawns, which swoop down to the cliffs. The house is one of 11 properties and landscapes owned by the Preservation Society of Newport County, which runs this and other mansion tours (401-847-1000; newportmansions.org).

5 *Rare Books* Noon

If the crowds haven't gotten to you yet, they soon will. Find an oasis at the **Redwood Library & Athenaeum** (50 Bellevue Avenue; 401-847-0292; redwoodlibrary.org), the oldest lending library in the United States. There's a collection of furniture, sculpture, and paintings, including six portraits signed by Gilbert Stuart. But even more charming is the Original Collection of 750 titles, purchased from England in 1748 by a group of Newport citizens. You may not always be able to just drop in to read them, but a look at the titles is an interesting window on the wide interests of the library's founders—from theology to bloodletting techniques to how to build a privy.

6 *Make Mine Gothic* 1 p.m.

Bannister's and Bowen's wharves, smack in the middle of Newport Harbor, make up ground zero for Newport's seafaring past. They are very scenic and wharfy. But you knew that. What you might not know is that many of the exteriors in a marvelous camp clas- sic, the gothic soap opera *Dark Shadows*, were shot in Newport. Have a salad at the **Black Pearl** (Bannister's Wharf; 401-846-5264; blackpearlnewport.com, $$), which was known as the Blue Whale in *Dark Shadows*.

ABOVE Harborside dining at Bannister's Wharf in the old Narragansett Bay port area, now transformed into a playground for vacationers, sailors, and summer residents.

RIGHT A rock wall along the Cliff Walk.

7 *Teak and Brass* 2 p.m.

Walk down to the **International Yacht Restoration School** (449 Thames Street; 401-848-5777; iyrs.org), which is both a center for restoring classic yachts and a school for history-minded craftsmen learning how to be restorers. There are heartbreakingly beautiful boats everywhere, in all stages of restoration. Make sure you wander through the turn-of-the-century factory building and out to the water, where you will find the school's most ambitious project, a 133-foot schooner, built in 1885, called *Coronet*. To see more, take a water taxi (newportharborshuttle.com) to the affiliated **Museum of Yachting** (moy.org), out on a bay island at Fort Adams State Park. Its exhibitions dovetail with the restoration work, explaining and expanding on what visitors see at the school.

8 *Back to the Wharf* 7 p.m.

Make an evening of it at the **Clarke Cooke House** (Banister's Wharf; clarkecooke.com), a lovely, rambling 18th-century house-turned-restaurant that covers all the bases for high-toned seaside night life. Start with drinks at its Midway Bar, and then, if you were feeling flush enough earlier to make a reservation, have dinner on the third floor at the airy and elegant **Porch** (401-849-2900; $$$), where you can watch the harbor below. Native lobster sautéed out of the shell requires no disassembly. Observe the patrons' variations on the dress code (gentlemen must wear collared shirts) and wait for the dancing at 11 p.m. Or invest a bit less and go down a floor and a half to the Candy Store, where you might try a huge crab cake served on New England brown bread.

SUNDAY

9 *Around the Dunes* 9 a.m.

You will need a salty wind to ruffle your hair today, something brisk and fresh to blow away all that dust and glitter. Head a few miles north out of town to the **Sachuest Wildlife Refuge** (769 Sachuest Point Road, Middletown; 401-847-5511; fws.gov/sachuestpoint). Its 242 acres of salt and freshwater marshes, sea grass, bayberry, and bittersweet and its rocky coastline are welcoming territory for all manner of wildlife, including seals, nesting terns, and harlequin ducks. Travel along the three-mile perimeter trail so you can be constantly on the water.

10 *In the Bay* 11 a.m.

For another perspective on Narragansett Bay, drive out onto the two-mile-long Claiborne Pell Bridge, which soars some 215 feet above the bay, and take the first exit, at Jamestown. This much smaller town is overshadowed by Newport, but its waterfront is worth a visit, with its own galleries, restaurants, and shops. Pick up some provisions, find the dock for the **Jamestown-Newport Ferry** (Conanicut Marina; 20 Narragansett Avenue; jamestownnewportferry.com), and park your car. Then ride the ferry to its first stop, Rose Island, and eat your lunch at the **Rose Island Lighthouse** (401-847-4242; roseisland.org). You'll find yourself in the middle of the bay, with gorgeous views of boats and sparkling water in every direction.

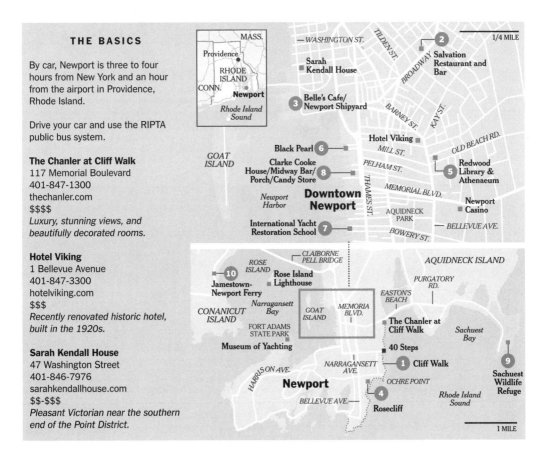

THE BASICS

By car, Newport is three to four hours from New York and an hour from the airport in Providence, Rhode Island.

Drive your car and use the RIPTA public bus system.

The Chanler at Cliff Walk
117 Memorial Boulevard
401-847-1300
thechanler.com
$$$$
Luxury, stunning views, and beautifully decorated rooms.

Hotel Viking
1 Bellevue Avenue
401-847-3300
hotelviking.com
$$$
Recently renovated historic hotel, built in the 1920s.

Sarah Kendall House
47 Washington Street
401-846-7976
sarahkendallhouse.com
$$-$$$
Pleasant Victorian near the southern end of the Point District.

Martha's Vineyard

What is it about presidents (at least Democratic ones) and Martha's Vineyard? The Kennedys have been coming since there were actual vineyards. The Clintons turned up nearly every summer of their White House years, and the Obamas followed. Wealthy A-listers usually hover nearby, hoping for invitations to the same parties where the first families show up. But part of the Vineyard's appeal is its easy way of shrugging off snobbery. Despite its popularity among the presidential set, this island, off Cape Cod in Massachusetts, is still a laid-back place with a lot of mopeds, fish shacks, and nice beaches. Folks here will tell you that the Vineyard is really just an old fishing community — that is, if you don't get stuck behind a motorcade. — DANIELLE PERGAMENT

FRIDAY

1 *Like a Kennedy* 2 p.m.

Martha's Vineyard is prettiest from the water, especially from the deck of a wooden sailboat with an American flag whipping off the stern. If you've ever wanted to know what it feels like to be a Kennedy or star in your own Ralph Lauren ad, you can charter a private sailboat through **Book A Boat** (508-645-2400; bookaboatmv.com). The company will arrange the place, type of boat, and all the particulars. For $50 to $75 a person, book a two-hour tour aboard a 40-foot boat. And don't be alarmed if the crew seems rather young. "I've been sailing here since I was a kid," one 19-year-old captain said reassuringly.

2 *Lobster Worship* 6 p.m.

Lobsters are practically a religion on the island, so it's fitting that some of the freshest are served in a church. On summer Fridays from 4:30 to 7:30 p.m., **Grace Church** in the tree-lined town of Vineyard Haven (Woodlawn Avenue and William Street; 508-693-0332; gracechurchmv.com) sets up picnic tables and sells lobster rolls — fresh, meaty cuts tossed lightly with mayonnaise and served on soft

hot dog buns. Judging by the long lines, the church-supper prices ($15 for lobster roll, chips, and a drink) might be the best deal in town. Sit with fellow worshipers, or take your meal down by the docks for a sunset view of the harbor.

3 *Secret Sweets* 9 p.m.

On summer nights, in a dark parking lot in the busier town of Oak Bluffs, a small crowd lines up at the screen door of the **Martha's Vineyard Gourmet Cafe and Bakery** (508-693-3688; 5 Post Office Square; mvbakery.com), waiting for warm doughnuts right out of the oven. The open secret is known as Back Door Donuts. The doughnuts are soft, sticky, and delicious, though veterans will tell you the apple fritters are superior.

SATURDAY

4 *Egg Rolls and Grandma's Jam* 9 a.m.

Get to the **West Tisbury Farmers' Market** (1067 State Road) when it opens at 9 so you can watch the stalls being set up — and shop before the best produce is picked over. Take your camera along on this expedition: you'll find the Vineyard farmers' market is a colorful scene of wildflowers, organic fruits and vegetables, homemade jams, and, somewhat curiously, a stall selling spicy Vietnamese egg rolls.

5 *Say Baaah* 10:30 a.m.

Martha's Vineyard is like a miniature Ireland — roads wind among bright green pastures where sheep, horses, and cattle graze, and many of the

OPPOSITE The Allen Sheep Farm & Wool Company, where even the livestock has an ocean view.

RIGHT The harbor at Oak Bluffs, a town of boats, beaches, and Victorian gingerbread houses.

farms welcome visitors. The **Allen Farm Sheep & Wool Company** in the bucolic town of Chilmark (421 South Road; 508-645-9064) has been run by the same family since 1762. Take in the views of rolling fields. Buy lamb chops or try on a handmade wool sweater in the gift shop. Those things grazing out front? They're lambs, and they're very friendly.

6 *Fried Goodness* 1 p.m.

It's a picture-perfect beach shack — without the beach. Housed in a tiny, weathered shingle house on a small side street in the old fishing port of Menemsha, the **Bite** (29 Basin Road; 508-645-9239; thebitemenemsha.com; $$) has been serving what many regard as the island's best fried clams, oysters, squid, shrimp, and scallops for more than 20 years. There are only two picnic tables, so bring a couple of icy beers, get a small order of clams, and take the paper bag of crispy deliciousness to the dock and watch the fishermen.

7 *Time in the Sand* 2 p.m.

The nicest beaches on Martha's Vineyard are private; you need a key to get in. But one that's open to the public is **Menemsha Beach**, a lovely stretch of sand just outside of town (ask for directions at the Bite; you're close). It is popular with families, and in the evening, it's a favorite place to watch the sunset. Swim a little, walk a little, or just hang out.

8 *Take a Hike* 4 p.m.

Yes, the Vineyard looks great from the water. But for a less-photographed view of the island's natural beauty, drive inland to **Waskosim's Rock Reservation** (mvlandbank.com), a nature reserve with 185 acres of open fields, wooded trails, and marshes. A modest, mile-long hike takes you to Waskosim's Rock, the boulder that divided the island between the English and Native American Wampanoag tribe 350 years ago. Tempting though it may be, resist climbing the rock — Vineyarders want to make sure it's around for another 350.

9 *State Dinner* 8 p.m.

It may not be as famous as the vegetable garden on Pennsylvania Avenue, but the herb and vegetable patch at the **State Road** restaurant (688 State Road; 508-693-8582; stateroadmv.com; $$) has its admirers. State Road features American cuisine using local ingredients. Inside, the place is simple and sleek — hardwood floors, high ceilings, and Edison bulb chandeliers. Look for the Island Farm to Table Plate, a selection of fingerling potatoes and seasonal vegetables from the restaurant garden, and pan-roasted sea scallops, locally caught, of course.

10 *Night at the Ritz* 11 p.m.

The island isn't known for night life, but your best bet for a nightcap is in the handful of lively bars

along Circuit Avenue in Oak Bluffs. Stop by the **Ritz Café** (4 Circuit Avenue; 508-693-9851), which attracts locals and has live music. Don't be fooled by the name — it's more of a draft beer than an appletini kind of joint.

SUNDAY

11 *Stores by the Seashore* 10 a.m.

There's a lot of good shopping between all those seagull paintings and dancing lobster napkins. In Vineyard Haven, drop by Carly Simon's **Midnight Farm** (18 Water-Cromwell Lane; 508-693-1997; midnightfarm.net) for its eclectic mix of gauzy sundresses, home furnishings, and, at times, signed copies of Simon's CDs. Up the street is **Nochi** (29

Main Street; 508-693-9074; nochimv.com), which sells robes, blankets, and all things cozy. And down the street is **LeRoux at Home** (62 Main Street; 508-693-0030; lerouxkitchen.com), a housewares store with a great selection of kitchen supplies including those dancing lobster napkins.

OPPOSITE The Menemsha Inn.

ABOVE The twice-a-week West Tisbury Farmer's Market attracts farmers and shoppers from all over the island.

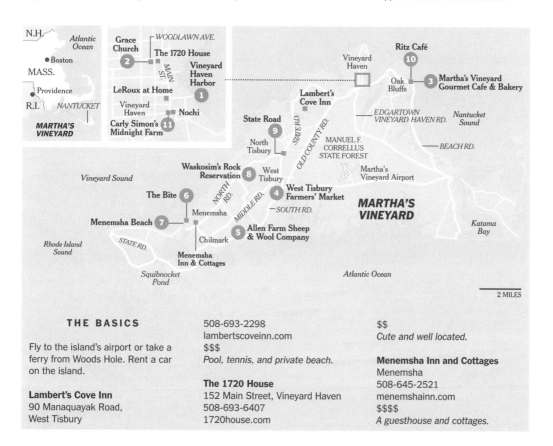

THE BASICS

Fly to the island's airport or take a ferry from Woods Hole. Rent a car on the island.

Lambert's Cove Inn
90 Manaquayak Road,
West Tisbury

508-693-2298
lambertscoveinn.com
$$$
Pool, tennis, and private beach.

The 1720 House
152 Main Street, Vineyard Haven
508-693-6407
1720house.com

$$
Cute and well located.

Menemsha Inn and Cottages
Menemsha
508-645-2521
menemshainn.com
$$$$
A guesthouse and cottages.

Nantucket

Near the beginning of Moby-Dick, *Ishmael explains why he decided to set sail from Nantucket: "There was a fine, boisterous something about everything connected with that famous old island." Today, more than a century and a half after it was written, that characterization still rings true. Though its downtown cobblestone streets and windswept fringes are now filled with expensive (some say exorbitant) restaurants and elegant cocktail bars, the island still has a swagger. To see it in full swing, linger over pints at one of the many harborside pubs, especially at sundown when sailors and fishing boats return to port.*
— BY SARAH GOLD

FRIDAY

1 *Historic Bearings* 3 p.m.

Main Street is lined with 19th-century storefronts and buckled brick sidewalks that seem to require deck shoes. To bone up on island history, visit **Mitchell's Book Corner** (54 Main Street; 508-228-1080; mitchellsbookcorner.com), a venerable four-decade-old bookstore. It has been renovated to include a spacious second floor that hosts weekly readings by local authors like Elin Hilderbrand and the National Book Award winner Nathaniel Philbrick. The beloved Nantucket Room remains, with hundreds of titles about island lore.

2 *Preppy It Up* 5 p.m.

You can still find a bona fide pair of the pinkish chinos called Nantucket Reds at **Murray's Toggery Shop** (62 Main Street; 508-228-0437; nantucketreds.com), and buy sunscreen or fancy bath products at **Nantucket Pharmacy** (45 Main Street; 508-228-0180), another classic of Nantucket shopping. But snappy new boutiques are always opening. One recent addition is **Jack Wills** (11 South Water Street; 508-332-1601; jackwills.com), the first stateside outpost of the British university outfitter, carrying jaunty polos, cable-knit sweaters, and canvas totes in signal-flag colors. Another is **Milly & Grace** (2 Washington

OPPOSITE Yachts rule in Nantucket Harbor, once the refuge of whaling ships.

RIGHT Brant Point Lighthouse in the harbor.

Street; 508-901-5051; millyandgrace.com), which sells bohemian-style caftans and tunics, cashmere sweaters, and embossed-silver jewelry.

3 *Fish of the Moment* 8 p.m.

Dune (20 Broad Street; 508-228-5550; dunenantucket.com; $$$) serves local seafood and produce in an intimate, warmly illuminated space. There are three dining rooms as well as a patio, but you'll need to book ahead. Changing menus have included dishes like flaky pan-roasted halibut fillet and minty spring-pea soup with tender baby shrimps. Stop by the petite quartzite bar on your way out.

4 *Beach Martinis* 10 p.m.

A young, tanned crowd fills the back room of **Galley Beach** (54 Jefferson Avenue; 508-228-9641; galleybeach.net; $$$). A cherished beachside restaurant, it has also become a late-night gathering spot since its 2008 renovation, serving drinks like pomegranate margaritas and the Seaside martini, made with Hendrick's gin and cucumber. By midnight the party spills outside, where tiki torches and sofas line the sand.

SATURDAY

5 *Island Market* 10 a.m.

Started in 2007, the **Nantucket Farmers & Artisans Market** (Cambridge and North Union Streets;

508-228-3399; sustainablenantucket.org) offers the wares of dozens of island farmers and artisans throughout the season and hosts workshops to encourage other would-be island growers and craftsmen. Keep an eye out for handmade quilts, freshly picked blueberries and raspberries, and fresh baked goods.

6 *Surf and Seals* Noon

If you're looking for a day of sand and saltwater and don't mind company, decamp to one of the favorite public swimming beaches, like Cisco Beach in the island's southwest, where strong waves draw surfers. But if you want to see a wilder and more natural Nantucket, drive out to the far west end, where the island tapers to the twin forks of Eel Point and Smith's Point. You'll need to rent a four-by-four — make sure it has a beach-driving permit; if not, you'll have to buy one for $150 at the Nantucket Police Station. You'll also need to reduce the tire pressure to maximize traction and minimize environmental damage. But after bumping along hillocky dune trails, you'll enter onto wide-open, mostly empty shores. There are no amenities to speak of, so bring all the supplies you'll need,

including food and water. Oh, and a camera. You might spot gray seals.

7 *Brew with a View* 5 p.m.

An afternoon of salty, sandy fun can leave you pretty thirsty. So it's convenient that the island's fabled west-end watering hole has reopened as **Millie's** (326 Madaket Road; 508-228-8435; milliesnantucket.com). Unlike its predecessor, the Westender, which closed a few years back, Millie's takes full advantage of the sunset location. A glassed-in second-floor bar lets you drink in panoramic vistas along with your Grey Lady or Whale's Tale Pale Ale, both from the Cisco Brewery a few miles down the road.

8 *Baja Style* 8 p.m.

Corazón del Mar (21 South Water Street; 508-228-0815; corazonnantucket.com; $$) has attracted a slavish following. This cozy, tiny papaya-orange den turns out south-of-the-border-inspired dishes like seascallop ceviche dressed in chili-citrus aji sauce or soft, Baja-style tacos filled with beer-battered cod, cabbage slaw, and spicy aioli. After dinner, take a stroll along Straight Wharf to **Nantucket Ice Cream** (44 Straight Wharf; 508-332-4949; nantucketicecream.com) for a cone or the house specialty: a sandwich of lemon sugar cookies and blueberry ice cream.

SUNDAY

9 *Sea Saviors* 10 a.m.

More than 700 shipwrecks litter the treacherous shoals and surrounding waters around Nantucket. For a fascinating glimpse into the island's underwater heritage, head to the **Nantucket Shipwreck & Lifesaving Museum** (158 Polpis Road; 508-228-1885; nantucketshipwreck.org). Reopened in 2009 after a $3 million expansion, the museum has vintage surfboats once used to save wreck survivors, childfriendly exhibits on Coast Guard sea dogs, and—most chillingly—grainy black-and-white 1956 film footage

BELOW Traditional weathered wooden shingles are everywhere, even on this luxury hotel, the White Elephant.

of one of the most infamous wrecks, the Italian ship *Andrea Doria*, shown slowly listing into the sea after its collision with a Swedish ocean liner.

10 *Beachside Brunch* Noon

The **Summer House Restaurant** in Siasconset village (17 Ocean Avenue; 508-257-9976; thesummerhouse.com; $$$$) is the island's most civilized spot for lunch, especially at its umbrella-shaded Beachside Bistro. Look for jazzed-up summertime classics like crab cake with corn salsa and tarragon aioli or a warm poached lobster salad with green beans and beurre blanc.

11 *Not Quite Open House* 1 p.m.

The **Bluff Walk** in Siasconset village was once the south shore's most fiercely guarded secret. But though you'll probably share the unmarked path with other visitors these days, a stroll here is still breathtaking. Pick up the trail in the village center (take a right and then a quick left at the end of Front Street) and walk along the high, Atlantic-skirting bluffs, past the backyards of some of the island's stateliest gray-shingled mansions. Erosion has left its mark (the last third of a mile, which used to extend all the way to Sankaty Head lighthouse, is now closed). But just stay on the path, keep your voice down and wear long pants — some residents, whether intentionally or not, let their sections become overgrown.

OPPOSITE ABOVE Windswept and far out to sea, Nantucket is rich in sandy spots for taking the sun.

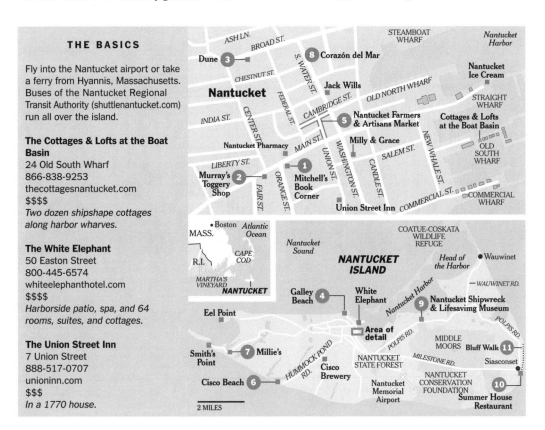

THE BASICS

Fly into the Nantucket airport or take a ferry from Hyannis, Massachusetts. Buses of the Nantucket Regional Transit Authority (shuttlenantucket.com) run all over the island.

The Cottages & Lofts at the Boat Basin
24 Old South Wharf
866-838-9253
thecottagesnantucket.com
$$$$
Two dozen shipshape cottages along harbor wharves.

The White Elephant
50 Easton Street
800-445-6574
whiteelephanthotel.com
$$$$
Harborside patio, spa, and 64 rooms, suites, and cottages.

The Union Street Inn
7 Union Street
888-517-0707
unioninn.com
$$$
In a 1770 house.

Provincetown

Park yourself anywhere on Commercial Street, the bustling main artery of Provincetown, and you will see celebrities, some real (John Waters, Paula Poundstone), some fake (that wasn't Cher). But mostly you will see ordinary people — lesbian, gay, bisexual, transgendered, and none of the above. Of the first 100 obvious couples to walk past Wired Puppy, a coffee-and-Wi-Fi joint, one typical summer night, 28 were female-female, 31 male-male, and 41 male-female. Four hundred years after the Pilgrims arrived here on the Mayflower, *water is still Provincetown's raison d'être — it provides the gorgeous scenery and the cod, sole, haddock, clams, lobsters, and oysters that make this a food lover's paradise. The trick, as in any resort town, is to eat at odd hours, which makes it possible to avoid crowds even on weekends. And then exercise. With great places to walk, bike, and swim, Provincetown makes burning calories as much fun as consuming them.* — BY FRED A. BERNSTEIN

FRIDAY

1 *On Two Wheels* 4 p.m.

Try to arrive in Provincetown by plane or boat. A car is useless in Provincetown, and besides, you can't really appreciate the place unless you see it as the Pilgrims saw it — on the ground, with the ocean out the front door and a vast bay out the back. Have the taxi driver take you straight to **Ptown Bikes** (42 Bradford Street; 508-487-8735; ptownbikes.com) for a reasonably priced bicycle rental. Then beat the evening crowd with an early trip to **Fanizzi's by the Sea** (539 Commercial Street; 508-487-1964; fanizzisrestaurant.com; $$), where you can find cold beer and the classic fish and chips, lightly battered fried clams, or a local fishermen's platter.

2 *Dune Buggin'* 5:30 p.m.

Time to burn off some of what you just ate. Ride your bike southwest to the end of Commercial Street, turn right at the traffic circle, and pedal till you see the Herring Cove Beach parking lot. At the end of the lot, a small opening in the fence leads to the bike trail into the **Province Lands** (nps.gov/caco). It's a five-foot-wide strip of asphalt that swoops up and down the dunes like a glorious doodle. It's about four miles to **Race Point Beach** — perhaps the town's most

breathtaking stretch of sand. Fill up at the water fountain and return to town in time for sunset.

3 *Night Galleries* 8 p.m.

Park your bike at the **Provincetown Art Association and Museum** (460 Commercial Street; 508-487-1750; paam.org). The town's premier art space, it grew with a smart addition by Machado and Silvetti (the architects of the Getty Villa restoration in Los Angeles). It's open till 10 p.m. (and free) on Friday nights. There are dozens of other galleries in Provincetown, and they, too, are open late on Fridays. Walk through the commercial district and drop in on a few.

4 *Love the Nightlife* 10 p.m.

The **Crown & Anchor** (247 Commercial Street; 508-487-1430; onlyatthecrown.com) offers one-stop shopping for gay entertainment. Arrayed around its courtyard are a disco with laser lights and throbbing speakers, a leather bar with hirsute habitués, a piano bar where everyone knows the lyrics, and more.

OPPOSITE Leave the car at home. Provincetown's main drag, Commercial Street, is best navigated on foot or by bicycle.

BELOW A trail ride down the Beech Forest Trail in the Province Lands area.

When the bars close at 1 a.m., follow the crowd to **Spiritus Pizza** (190 Commercial Street; 508-487-2808; spirituspizza.com; $). Some call it the "sidewalk sale" — the last chance for a hookup — but really it's

ABOVE The West End, at Provincetown Harbor.

BELOW Provincetown is on the East Coast, but its location at the end of curving Cape Cod makes it a good place for watching sunsets, like this one at Herring Cove Beach.

a giant block party. The pizza, with thin crust and more marinara than cheese, is super.

SATURDAY

5 *Window Seat* 10 a.m.
    If your hotel doesn't have breakfast, head to **Cafe Heaven** (199 Commercial Street; 508-487-9639; $$) for delicious omelets, homemade granola, and banana pancakes. From behind its big windows, you can peruse the local papers for concert and theater listings.

6 *Stairway after Heaven* 11:30 a.m.
    You loved those pancakes. Now work them off. Head to the **Pilgrim Monument**, a gray stone crenellated tower that has looked out over the town and out to sea since 1910 (pilgrim-monument.org). Buy a bottle of water from the machine outside and then start climbing; a mix of stairs and ramps will take you to the top of the 252-foot tower. On a clear day, you can see the tops of Boston's tallest buildings.

7 *The End of Cape Cod* 1 p.m.
    Head to **Angel Foods** in the East End (467 Commercial Street; 508-487-6666; angelfoods.com) for takeout — ask for the delicious lobster cakes and a savory curry chicken salad. With lunch in your backpack, ride to the traffic circle at the end of Commercial

Street and lock your bike to the split-rail fence. Walk out onto the breakwater, a 1.2-mile-long line of rocks the size of automobiles. After a spectacular 25-minute trek, you'll find yourself on a deserted beach.

8 *Retail Corridor* 4 p.m.

Time for some shopping. **Wa** (220 Commercial Street; 508-487-6355; waharmony.com) is a shop that looks more like a perfectly curated museum of Asian art and furniture. **Forbidden Fruit** (173 Commercial Street; 508-487-9800; eatmyapple.com) sells unusual home decor items that run from funky to bizarre, including shiny masks with a slightly carnal tone. At **Alice Brock Studio** (69 Commercial Street; 508-487-2127; alicebrock.com), you may meet the proprietor, who sells her artwork here. It's not her first commercial venture—she is the Alice immortalized by Arlo Guthrie in the song *Alice's Restaurant*.

BELOW The view from Cape Cod Bay inland toward Commercial Street and the town center.

9 *Master of Margaritas* 9:30 p.m.

The dinner crowds are thinning; now it's time to eat. Try **Lorraine's** (133 Commercial Street; 508-487-6074; $$), a nouvelle Mexican restaurant where the margarita menu offers a vast selection of tequilas in price ranges from under $10 to closer to $75. Try the crab enchiladas or tuna tacos. Or if you've overdosed on seafood, look for choices like rack of lamb and filet mignon. Vegetarians will survive here, too, with plenty of rice, vegetables, and cheese in Mexican-style combinations.

SUNDAY

10 *Portuguese Breakfast* 10 a.m.

This time, breakfast at **Chach** (73 Shank Painter Road; 508-487-1530; $$), an update on the diner theme with a retro checkered floor and vinyl booths. There are plenty of typical breakfast choices, and this is a good place for Portuguese sweet bread, a nod to the Portuguese fishermen

The tour ventures out into the sand dunes on protected lands at the tip of Cape Cod, and will take you past dune shacks where writers and artists like Eugene O'Neill, Jack Kerouac, Tennessee Williams, and Jackson Pollock once spent summers working in near total isolation. The dunes are a magical experience, and the guides are happy to share their knowledge about the people who once lived here and the hardy plants and wildlife that find sustenance in this remote and windy spot.

who once dominated this town. The abundant cod that sustained them are largely fished out, but some of those fishermen's descendants remain, and Provincetown celebrates their traditions with its Portuguese Festival every summer.

11 *The Windblown Shore* 1 p.m.
Take a guided trip by S.U.V. through the **Cape Cod National Seashore** with **Art's Dune Tours** (4 Standish Street; 508-487-1950; artsdunetours.com).

ABOVE Wa, an Asian-themed shop on Commercial Street.

OPPOSITE Although Provincetown today is anything but austere, the Pilgrim Monument celebrates its Puritan roots.

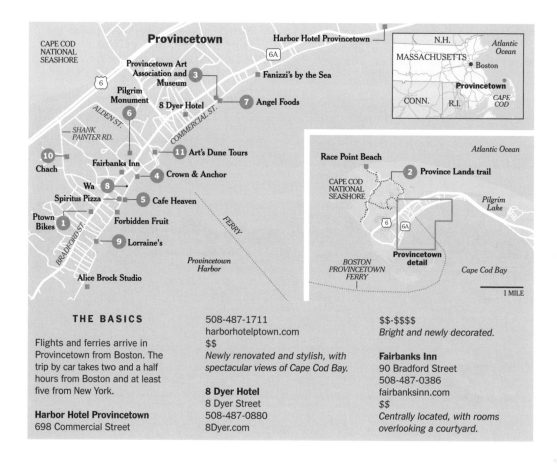

THE BASICS

Flights and ferries arrive in Provincetown from Boston. The trip by car takes two and a half hours from Boston and at least five from New York.

Harbor Hotel Provincetown
698 Commercial Street

508-487-1711
harborhotelptown.com
$$
Newly renovated and stylish, with spectacular views of Cape Cod Bay.

8 Dyer Hotel
8 Dyer Street
508-487-0880
8Dyer.com

$$-$$$$
Bright and newly decorated.

Fairbanks Inn
90 Bradford Street
508-487-0386
fairbanksinn.com
$$
Centrally located, with rooms overlooking a courtyard.

Boston

Boston is known for its bricks and brownstones, but with downtown stretching unimpeded to the water-front after the $15 billion Big Dig, these days it feels like a whole new city. High-tech exuberance, modern parks, and a reclaimed harbor add to the sheen of newness, complementing the youthful energy of the large student population. There's no danger that the city will forget its pivotal role in American history. The Freedom Trail is still there for the walking, and stately colonial houses still invite a stroll in Beacon Hill. But Boston offers some new paths to travel, too.
— BY KATIE ZEZIMA

FRIDAY

1 *Everything Old Is New* 4:30 p.m.

In a city this historic, it's not every day that a new neighborhood is built from scratch. But that is essentially the story with Fan Pier, a former area of industrial blight on the South Boston waterfront being slowly transformed into a hub of fashion, art, and dining. Anchored by the **Institute of Contemporary Art** (100 Northern Avenue; 617-478-3100; icaboston.org), a glass-and-steel museum that seems to hover over the harbor, it is a go-to place for the cool crowd. Shopping's a draw, too: **LouisBoston** (60 Northern Avenue; 617-262-6100; louisboston.com), the high-end store, has a 20,000-square-foot flagship, with a restaurant, next to the museum.

2 *Taste of Dakar* 8 p.m.

There's more on Boston dinner plates than baked beans. As the city becomes more diversified, so do its culinary offerings. Case in point: **Teranga** (1746 Washington Street; 617-266-0003; terangaboston.com; $), a Senegalese restaurant that opened in May 2009 on a busy South End street, far from the well-dressed masses. An elegant space with exposed brick walls and a long banquette, it serves spicy, fragrant dishes like nems, spring rolls stuffed with vermicelli, and thiébou

djeun, a popular West African dish with kingfish, jasmine rice, tomato sauce, carrots, and cabbage.

3 *Hear the Buzz* 10 p.m.

There are plenty of places to catch a show but not so many to hear live music with no cover. The **Beehive** (541 Tremont Street; 617-423-0069; beehiveboston.com), a restaurant where the lights are low and bands are chill, fills the void. Descend the staircase to be closer to the band, or stick to the quieter bar upstairs. Either way, don't leave without catching the intricate, hand-painted bathroom walls.

SATURDAY

4 *Easy as Green* 11 a.m.

Downtown was once defined by an elevated steel highway. Then by the Big Dig, the seemingly never-ending project to sink the roadway underground. After billions of dollars and untold numbers of delays, it is finally home to the **Rose Kennedy Greenway** (rosekennedygreenway.org), a mile-long ribbon of lawns, public art, and much-needed playgrounds snaking along Atlantic Avenue. To explore this emerald oasis, start at South Station and meander toward the North End, stopping to frolic in the fountains or take a spin on the carousel. At **Christopher Columbus Park**, find a spot under a wisteria-covered trellis and watch as boats bob in the harbor and planes take off from Logan Airport. It was worth the wait.

5 *Lobster Bar* 1 p.m.

It's a cliché for a reason: you can't visit Boston, smell a salt breeze, and not want to eat seafood.

OPPOSITE The landmark Custom House Tower, now a Marriott hotel, overlooking the Rose Kennedy Greenway in Boston.

RIGHT Wharf District Park, one of the interconnected public spaces along the Rose Kennedy Greenway.

Steer clear of the waterfront traps and head to **Neptune Oyster** (63 Salem Street; 617-742-3474; neptuneoyster.com; $$$), a tiny spot where Sam Adams-swilling frat boys rub shoulders with fabulous Champagne sippers at the marble bar. The attraction? Why, the lobster roll, a mountain of warm, butter-slicked lobster piled into a soft brioche bun, with a side of crispy skin-on fries.

6 *Couture and Cannolis* 3 p.m.

The North End, Boston's Italian neighborhood, is now as much Milan as manicotti, with boutiques popping up between restaurants and pastry shops. **Acquire** (61 Salem Street; 857-362-7380; acquireboutique.com)

melds vintage and modern housewares; the **Velvet Fly** (28 Parmenter Street; 617-557-4359; thevelvetfly.com) does the same with indie designers and old threads. In the continuing battle between women and the perfect jeans, the ladies win at **In.jean.ius** (441 Hanover Street; 617-523-5326; injeanius.com), where the friendly staff stops at nothing to turn up that perfect pair.

7 *Personalized Libations* 6 p.m.

Tired of forking over $15 for a cocktail that doesn't quite speak to your individual tastes? Then pull up to **Drink** (348 Congress Street; 617-695-1806; drinkfortpoint.com), where mixology becomes personal. Instead of providing menus, bartenders ask patrons about their tastes and liquors of choice, and try to concoct the perfect tincture. The bar is reminiscent of a booze-drenched chemistry lab, and any experiments that don't turn out right can be sent back. You can't go wrong with the Maximilian Affair, a smoky combination of mezcal, St. Germain, Punt e Mes, and lemon juice.

8 *Provence on the Charles* 8 p.m.

Boston raised its culinary game with **Bistro du Midi** (272 Boylston Street; 617-426-7878;

ABOVE AND LEFT The 1909 main building and the Foster + Partners-designed American wing, opened a century later, of the venerable Museum of Fine Arts Boston.

bistrodumidi.com; $$$), run by Robert Sisca, formerly the executive sous chef at the renowned New York restaurant Le Bernardin. Here Sisca has created a Provençal menu with a focus on local fish. Ask to be seated upstairs, where businessmen and dolled-up couples sit in buttery yellow leather chairs and gaze at unbeatable views of the Public Garden outside.

9 *Local Tallboys* 10:30 p.m.

Tourists flock to the "Cheers" bar at 84 Beacon Street, made famous by the television series. But there's an antidote around the corner at **75 Chestnut** (75 Chestnut Street; 617-227-2175; 75chestnut.com). Tucked on a romantic side street, this dimly lighted restaurant feels like a modern take on an old brownstone, with tin ceilings and mahogany pillars. For a younger and cooler scene, check out the **Delux Café** (100 Chandler Street; 617-338-5258), a reigning temple of kitsch with walls decorated with records, comic books, and a bust of Elvis. To get some New England hipster cred, order a tallboy Narragansett Beer, the region's answer to Pabst Blue Ribbon.

SUNDAY

10 *Morning Hash* 10 a.m.

Put your sunglasses on and grab an outdoor seat at the **Woodward**, a restaurant and tavern at the Ames Hotel (1 Court Street; 617-979-8200;

woodwardatames.com; $$$) that is injecting minimalist style into the staid Financial District. Brunch offers modern New England fare, like lobster and leek hash, along with great people-watching.

11 *Art and Architects* Noon

Boston has had a first-rate art collection, spread over its well-known museums, for as long as anyone

TOP The Institute of Contemporary Art in Fan Pier, a new go-to neighborhood in South Boston. The museum's glass-and-steel cantilever hovers over the harbor.

ABOVE Custom mixologists at Drink, a South Boston bar.

can remember. Lately, renowned architects have arrived in town to design more display space. The old Fogg Museum, across the Charles River at Harvard, closed to make way for a larger building by Renzo Piano, to open in 2013. Piano also designed new breathing space for the quirky **Isabella Stewart Gardner Museum** (280 The Fenway; 617- 566-1401; gardnermuseum.org), although its masterpieces must remain in the Venetian-style palazzo where Ms. Gardner installed them. To see art and architecture

newly blended at the venerable **Museum of Fine Arts** (465 Huntington Avenue; 617-267-9300; mfa.org), head to its Art of the Americas wing by Foster + Partners, which opened in 2010. The I.M. Pei-designed galleries added in the 1980s are still worth a look, too. Prefer a ballgame to a museum trip? If it's baseball season and the Red Sox are in town, take in a game at **Fenway Park** (4 Yawkey Way; redsox.com), the beloved ballpark that remains right where it was when it opened in 1912.

ABOVE Fenway Park, home of the Boston Red Sox.

OPPOSITE Sailboats in the fleet of Community Boating Inc. on the Charles River Esplanade.

THE BASICS

Fly to Logan Airport or take a high-speed Amtrak train from New York.

Public transporation is plentiful (mbta.com).

The W Boston
100 Stuart Street
617-261-8700
whotels.com/boston
$$$-$$$$
Opened in 2009, with 235 sleek rooms overlooking the Theater District.

The Ames Hotel
1 Court Street
617-979-8100
ameshotel.com
$$$
Also new in 2009. Minimalist rooms and trendy décor.

Newbury Guest House
261 Newbury Street
617-437-7666
newburyguesthouse.com
$$
A brownstone with quaint touches and 32 rooms.

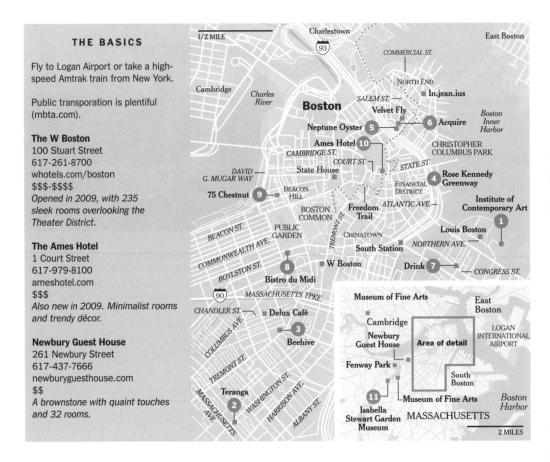

Cambridge

Home of Harvard and the Massachusetts Institute of Technology, with a quarter of its 100,000-plus residents enrolled at one or the other, Cambridge, Massachusetts, has a well-deserved reputation as the country's academic epicenter. The life of the mind comes with plenty of perks: a collection of arty cinemas, a thriving music scene, scads of independent bookshops, and a smorgasbord of international restaurants. Though Harvard Square is the tourist center, other neighborhoods offer visitors respites from both its escalating gentrification and its Ivy League self-regard. The grittier Central Square is home to great clubs and cheap, sophisticated ethnic restaurants, and Inman Square is young and adventurous. — BY POOJA BHATIA

FRIDAY

1 *Pizza cum Laude* 7 p.m.

Locals usually delight in dissing all things Yale, but for some reason they defer to New Haven when it comes to pizza. There's really no need. The patrons lining up for seats at **Emma's** (40 Hampshire Street; 617-864-8534; emmaspizza.com; $) say it slings the best pies in the Northeast, with crackling, wafer-thin crusts; about 30 interesting but not-too-outré toppings; and the ideal crust-sauce-cheese ratio. Design your own pie; one winning combination is goat cheese, basil, thyme-roasted mushrooms, and roasted tomatoes. For some heat, try rosemary sauce, hot cherry peppers, and Italian sweet sausage. Don't overdo it. Your next stop is dessert.

2 *Creativity on Ice* 9 p.m.

Cantabrigians take their ice cream seriously. Many profess to the molto-rich versions at Toscanini's; frozen yogurt lovers lean to BerryLine. But foodies in the know flock to **Christina's** (1255 Cambridge Street; 617-492-7021; christinasicecream.com), where adzuki bean and ginger molasses are among the dozens of flavors and a scoop of khulfi accurately

translates the cardamom-rich Indian treat. Purists, be content: Christina's has good old vanilla, chocolate, and strawberry, too.

3 *Time to Improvise* 10 p.m.

Catch the second set at the dark, intimate **Regattabar** at the Charles Hotel (1 Bennett Street; 617-661-5000; regattabarjazz.com), which has long been the leading jazz spot in town—and some who have said that weren't talking only about Cambridge, but about Boston as well. Fans of jazz, blues, soul, R&B, and world music also venture across the Charles River to Allston to catch their favorites at **Scullers Jazz Club** (400 Soldiers Road; 617-783-0090; scullersjazz.com) in the Doubletree Hotel. Both spots book nationally known musicians.

SATURDAY

4 *Pass the Jam* 10 a.m.

Toast, French or traditional from homemade breads, isn't the only choice at the **Friendly Toast** (1 Kendall Square, Building 200; 617-621-1200; thefriendlytoast.net; $$), a breakfast favorite steps from M.I.T. Eggs in many permutations, pancakes decorated with coconut and chocolate chips, and plain Belgian waffles are all on the extensive menu. If the excesses of last night's student-style dinner were too much, try the fruit salad with granola.

5 *Getting Beyond Euclid* 11 a.m.

At M.I.T., Cambridge's "other" university, numbers are king. They denote classes ("I've got

OPPOSITE An autumn regatta on the Charles River near the campus of Harvard University.

RIGHT A courtyard view of the Frank Gehry-designed Stata Center at the Massachusetts Institute of Technology.

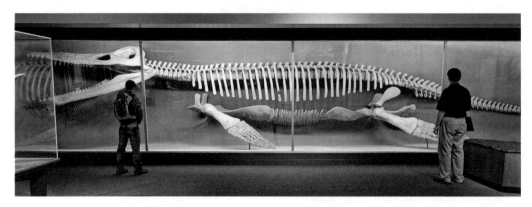

6012" means you're headed to microelectronic devices and circuits) and even majors (8, for instance, is physics), and most buildings on the largely undistinguished campus are known by them. But some recent additions have not only names but also architectural verve. The undergrads living in **Simmons Hall** (229-243 Vassar Street), designed by Steven Holl, say it reminds them of a waffle or sponge, thanks to the 5,500 cut-out windows that give it a porous look. Just down the road is Frank Gehry's fanciful **Stata Center** (32 Vassar Street). Orange brick portions pay humorous homage to M.I.T.'s boxy engineering labs, but they're cut up by aluminum waves, lacking right angles, that resemble the pleats of a skirt or a chef's toque.

6 *Food for Curiosity* Noon

You're at M.I.T., so don't miss the **MIT Museum** (265 Massachusetts Avenue; 617-253-5927; web.mit.edu/museum) 15,000 square feet of inviting ongoing and rotating exhibits that will absorb anyone who likes to ask "Why?" or "How does it work?" Visit Kismet, the sociable robot; step into the nucleus of a cell to watch DNA do its job; and tilt your head to see the shimmering changeability of some of the museum's hundreds of 3-D holograms. Look for gizmos like the

"Remarkable Double Piddler Hydraulic Happening Machine," which uses a strobe light to deconstruct a water stream into individual droplets.

7 *The World in a Square* 3 p.m.

Give Harvard equal time with a walk in Harvard Yard, and then turn your attention to Harvard Square. Chain restaurants call it home these days, but so do quirky street performers, plotting chess masters, texting teenagers, and independent bookstores holding out against the tide of online book buying that has swamped so many of their number. Book lovers should plan to spend some serious time at the **Harvard Book Store** (1256 Massachusetts Avenue; 617-661-1515; harvard.com), which has been around for nearly 80 years and has an outstanding selection of books to suit every interest, as well as a solid used-book section. A half-block away, the **Grolier Poetry Book Shop** (6 Plympton Street; 617-547-4648; grolierpoetrybookshop.org) is a destination for poets and scholars from around the world. If you're looking for Camus or Cervantes in the original language, head to **Schoenhof's Foreign Books** (76A Mount Auburn Street, 617-547-8855; schoenhofs.com).

8 *The View at Dinner* 8 p.m.

The decor alone is reason enough to visit the **Soiree Room** at **UpStairs on the Square** (91 Winthrop Street; 617-864-1933; upstairsonthesquare.com; $$$). Begin your gawking at the leopard-print carpet and work your way up along the walls, painted à la Klimt, to the gilded mirror ceiling. Somehow it all adds up to whimsical charm. The food, like poached Atlantic salmon or lobster bouillabaisse, can be as luxe as the furnishings, but even the humblest dishes are well tended. Tasting menus are both standard and vegetarian.

9 *Nightclub Nightcap* 9:30 p.m.

With Persianesque drapings on its platforms and divans, the **Enormous Room** (567 Massachusetts Avenue; 617-491-5599; enormous.tv) lets you lie down and absorb the atmosphere — that is, if you can find the unlabeled entrance. (Hint: Look for the elephant silhouette.) With a North African vibe and reliable D.J.'s, this bar attracts would-be bohemians — though the high-priced cocktails can require a trust fund. On most Saturday nights the place fills up by 10.

SUNDAY

10 *Riverside* 11 a.m.

Six days a week, cars choke Memorial Drive on the banks of the Charles River. On Sundays from the end of April to mid-November the road closes to cars and fills up with runners, walkers, in-line skaters, and cyclists, all eager to burn off weekend excesses. The

route, punctuated by boathouses, parks, and geese, is lovely in any season, especially when the sun shines and the river sparkles under an azure sky. If you'd like to get out on the river yourself, cross the river to Boston and rent a kayak at **Community Boating** (21 David G. Mugar Way, Boston; 617-523-1038; community-boating.org). Paddle out for some of the best views to be had of both Boston and Cambridge.

OPPOSITE ABOVE The skeleton of a Kronosaurus queenslandicus at the Harvard Natural History Museum.

OPPOSITE BELOW Nightlife at the Enormous Room, where the atmosphere feels bohemian but the cocktail prices might shock a starving artist.

THE BASICS

Cambridge is a 15-minute cab ride from Logan International Airport in Boston. Parking is a nightmare. Plan on plenty of walking.

Hotel Veritas
1 Remington Street
617-520-5000
thehotelveritas.com
$$$
New but intentionally old-looking 31-room hotel just east of Harvard Square. Free passes to a nearby yoga studio and gym.

Charles Hotel
One Bennett Street
617-864-1200
charleshotel.com
$$$
Close to Harvard's quads and the Kennedy School of Government.

Hotel Marlowe
25 Edwin H. Land Boulevard
800-825-7140
hotelmarlowe.com
$$-$$$$
A Kimpton boutique hotel in East Cambridge.

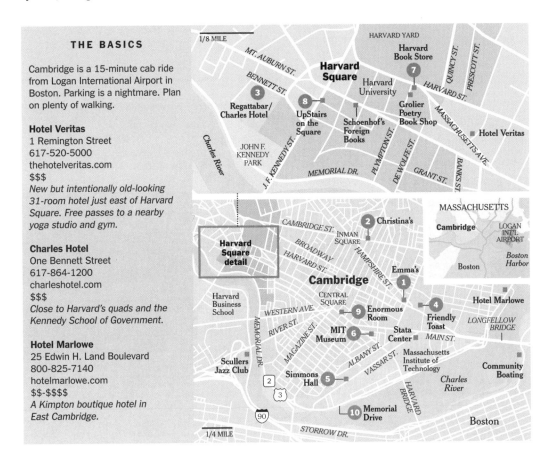

Portsmouth

Driving into town, it is hard to miss the fact that Portsmouth is still a working deep-water port, the seafaring hub of New Hampshire's 18-mile slice of Atlantic coast. But Market Street also leads to a charming downtown filled with eccentric and upscale shops, galleries, and restaurants. That's the Portsmouth paradox: It's a seacoast getaway town without a beach, an escapist retreat with a decidedly real-world spin. It's also scenic. Settled in 1623, Portsmouth grew as a shipbuilding center, making wood-masted ships for the King's Navy. Four fires in the first half of the 1800s led the residents to build with brick, creating a legacy of remarkable 19th-century city architecture including the white-steepled North Church, the town landmark.
— BY DAVID A. KELLY

FRIDAY

1 *Tugboat City* 6 p.m.

A working harbor means tugboats, which in Portsmouth are often docked downtown, along the side of Ceres Street. The blunt-nosed red and black Moran tugs are used to guide ships up and down the swift currents and winding channels of the Piscataqua River. For the tugboat-obsessed (or anyone who likes nautical gifts), a visit to nearby **Tugboat Alley** (47 Bow Street; 603-430-9556; tugboatalley.com) is in order. In addition to everything tugboat, the store offers harbor tours aboard the six-passenger *Tug Alley Too.*

2 *Dinner on the Deck* 7 p.m.

Portsmouth's tugboats also make a great back-drop for an outdoor dinner. Explore the waterfront decks and bars along the back of Bow Street. **Poco's Bow Street Cantina** (37 Bow Street; 603-431-5967; pocosbowstreetcantina.com; $) has a usually packed bar area as well as outdoor seating. The menu mixes Mexico and New England with dishes like lobster quesadilla and lobster salad tacos. The **River House** (53 Bow Street; 603-431-2600; riverhouse53bow.com;

OPPOSITE North Church, on Market Square, is part of Portsmouth's well-kept legacy of 19th-century brick buildings.

RIGHT Despite its name, the Portsmouth Naval Shipyard is just across the Piscataqua River in Kittery, Maine.

$$) serves up casual entrees along with great deck views of the river and the bridge across it to Maine. On a warm summer night, you may have to wait for a table.

3 *Watering Hole* 9 p.m.

For a peek into the past, stop by the **Spring Hill Tavern** (15 Bow Street; 603-431-5222), just below the **Dolphin Striker** restaurant (dolphinstriker.com). At the far end of the low-slung bar is a freshwater spring (now under glass) in an old brick well where the early mariners filled up their freshwater reserves. You can soak up your own refreshments while listening to one of the blues, jazz, and rock bands that play almost every night.

4 *A Bite Before Bed* Midnight

When the bars empty out, Gilley's fills up. It doesn't take long for a line of 20 or 30 people to snake out the door of this moveable 1940 diner, the latest of a series of food trailers here dating to a horse-drawn cart in 1912. **Gilley's PM Lunch** (175 Fleet Street; 603-431-6343; gilleyspmlunch.com) feeds Portsmouth until 2:30 a.m. with fare like hamburgers or kraut dogs, for about $3 each, and chocolate milk.

SATURDAY

5 *Water, Water Everywhere* 10 a.m.

Visiting Portsmouth without going out on the water is almost a sin. Boat trips with **Portsmouth Harbor Cruises** (64 Ceres Street Dock; 603-436-8084; portsmouthharbor.com) go into the harbor and beyond. The Isles of Shoals cruise will take you

to a group of colorfully named islands (Peavey's, Smuttynose) six miles off shore. They were explored by Captain John Smith of Pocahontas fame, and the pirate Blackbeard lurked among them—he is said to have left behind a buried treasure of silver bars.

6 *Island with a View* 1 p.m.

For a nice picnic spot and a good viewpoint toward the Portsmouth Naval Shipyard across the river in Kittery, Maine, drive out to **Peirce Island** (seacoastnh.com/Travel/Scenic_Walks/Peirce_Island/). Park and walk over the causeway to Four Tree Island. Unroll a blanket, unpack a picnic lunch, and watch the big tankers roll in. The shipyard dates to 1800; John Paul Jones's ship, *Ranger*, was built there. These days the yard overhauls, services, and refuels nuclear-powered submarines.

7 *Past and Present* 2 p.m.

Back across the bridge lies **Prescott Park**, a stretch of pretty waterfront that in the late 1800s and early 1900s was home to brothels and bars popular with sailors from the shipyard. These days it fills with crowds for the performances of the Prescott Park Arts Festival (prescottpark.org), featuring musical comedy and concerts in genres from jazz to folk and country. Nearby in **Strawbery Banke** (14 Hancock Street; 603-433-1100; strawberybanke.org), one of the country's most unusual outdoor museums, costumed role-players re-create Portsmouth life from the 1600s to the 20th century. Visitors find themselves chatting with an 18th-century storekeeper and then walking down a few doors to a 1950s living room with Roy Rogers and Dale Evans on the television set.

8 *Life on the Square* 5 p.m.

Market Square and nearby streets are lined with shops and galleries good for browsing and gift buying. For a cappuccino and some people-watching, hunt for an outdoor table at **Breaking New Grounds** (14 Market Square; 603-436-9555), a coffee shop frequented by everyone from business types to artists. At some point your eyes will also be drawn to the brick facade and towering chimneys of the **Portsmouth Athenaeum** (9 Market Square; 603-431-2538; portsmouthathenaeum.org), built in 1805. Inside is one of the oldest private libraries in the United States, a repository of local history including a research library and exhibition gallery that are both open to the public a few days each week.

9 *Brick Bistro* 8 p.m.

Expect to find seasonal ingredients at **Black Trumpet Bistro** (29 Ceres Street; 603-431-0887; blacktrumpetbistro.com; $$-$$$), which pledges that its menu changes every six weeks. The building dates to the early 19th century, with brick walls, hand-hewn beams in the upstairs wine bar, and windows overlooking the river. Contemporary takes on steak and seafood entrees enlist accompaniments like cactus-poblano hashcakes and cipollini onions, and the updated New England desserts may include ginger-bread pineapple upside-down cake with mango coulis.

SUNDAY

10 *Next Door Harbor* 10 a.m.

Pick up coffee at the **Works Bakery Cafe** (9 Congress Street; 603-431-4434; worksbakerycafe.com). Then get in the car and drive a few miles down the

BELOW Street music on a hammer dulcimer.

coast to Rye, a part-rural, part-seaside town whose affluent residents have included the writer Dan Brown and Senator Scott Brown of Massachusetts. At **Rye Harbor State Park** (1730 Ocean Boulevard, Rye; 603-436-1552; nhstateparks.org/explore/state-parks/rye-harbor-state-park.aspx), settle on a bench and enjoy the views of the harbor and the Isles of Shoals.

11 *But Did They Drink Mimosas?* Noon
Have a lavish brunch at **Wentworth by the Sea** (588 Wentworth Road, New Castle; 603-422-7322; $$$), a grand Victorian hotel with sea views from the dining room and outdoor deck. A place this old has to have some history, and the Wentworth does. It was already 30 years old when Russian and Japanese

delegates stayed there in 1905, brought together by President Theodore Roosevelt to negotiate the end of the Russo-Japanese War. They cemented their agreement in the Treaty of Portsmouth, and Roosevelt won the Nobel Peace Prize.

OPPOSITE ABOVE Red brick and coffee on Congress Street.

ABOVE Tour boats cruise in the harbor and venture to offshore islands that were once a pirates' hideout.

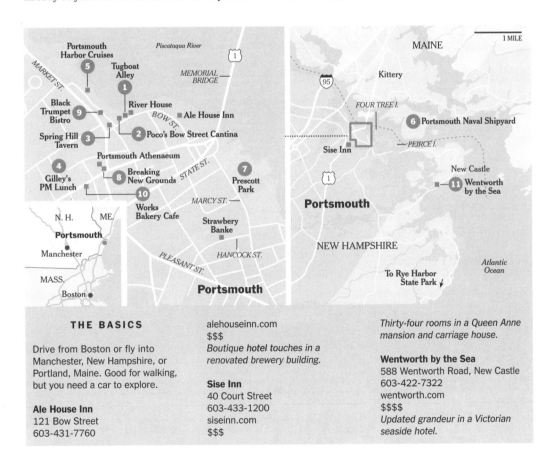

THE BASICS

Drive from Boston or fly into Manchester, New Hampshire, or Portland, Maine. Good for walking, but you need a car to explore.

Ale House Inn
121 Bow Street
603-431-7760

alehouseinn.com
$$$
Boutique hotel touches in a renovated brewery building.

Sise Inn
40 Court Street
603-433-1200
siseinn.com
$$$

Thirty-four rooms in a Queen Anne mansion and carriage house.

Wentworth by the Sea
588 Wentworth Road, New Castle
603-422-7322
wentworth.com
$$$$
Updated grandeur in a Victorian seaside hotel.

Portland Maine

Portland is known for three L's: lobster, lighthouses, and L.L. Bean (O.K., make that four L's). Here's another: local. In recent years, this city on the coast of Maine has welcomed a wave of locavore restaurants, urban farms, and galleries that feature local artists. Abandoned brick warehouses are being repurposed as eco-friendly boutiques. In the main square, a 19th-century building has been refashioned into a farmers' market. And everywhere you look, this once-sleepy industrial town is showing signs of rejuvenation, usually by keeping things local.
— BY LIONEL BEEHNER

FRIDAY

1 *The Artsy Crowd* 4 p.m.

To see bohemian Portland, stroll down Congress Street, where at least a dozen galleries, studios, and cafes have opened in recent years. David Marshall, a beret-wearing painter who moonlights as a city councilman, is among the artists who exhibit at **Constellation Gallery** (511 Congress Street; 207-409-6617; constellationart.com). An artsy crowd can be found at **Local Sprouts** (649 Congress Street; 207-899-3529; localsproutscooperative.com), an earthy, community-supported cafe as crunchy as it sounds. Down the street is the **Portland Public Library** (5 Monument Square; 207-871-1700; portlandlibrary.com), which has revamped its gallery and added an atrium.

2 *Made in Maine* 7 p.m.

Portland's locavore scene has blossomed in recent years, as evidenced by attention to it on the Food Network. Among the most talked about restaurants is **Farmer's Table** (205 Commercial Street; 207-347-7479; farmerstablemaine.com; $$), which offers nice terrace views of the harbor. The owner and chef, Jeff Landry, gets his vegetables from area gardens and serves dishes like beef short ribs from grass-fed cows reared on a nearby farm. Or try **Caiola's** (58 Pine Street; 207-772-1110; caiolas.com; $$), a locals' favorite serving Mediterranean fare.

3 *Indie Playground* 9 p.m.

Live music anchors Portland's night life. The **State Theatre** (609 Congress Street; 207-956-6000; statetheatreportland.com), a Depression-era movie house that closed in 2006, reopened as a concert hall in 2010, drawing touring bands like Bright Eyes and Hinder. Music buffs also make their way to the **Port City Music Hall** (504 Congress Street; 207-899-4990; portcitymusichall.com), a club glitzy by Portland standards that even lifts a velvet rope for its V.I.P.'s. A younger, more relaxed crowd flocks to **Space Gallery** (538 Congress Street; 207-828-5600; space538.org), scruffy art space by day and indie rock music spot by night.

SATURDAY

4 *Suburban Bagels* 8:30 a.m.

Across a drawbridge lies South Portland, a city of bungalows with a quiet beach. But the sweetest reason to visit is the **Scratch Baking Co.** (416 Preble Street, South Portland; 207-799-0668; scratchbakingco.com; $), a bakery on Willard Square that sells oven-fresh muffins, scones, and sourdough bagels. Get there before 9 a.m., as the bagels run out fast. Then snag a spot on Willard Beach, a patch of rocky sand with views of the coast.

OPPOSITE Taking in the view from Peaks Island, an easy ferry ride from town and a good place to explore by bicycle. Rent one at Brad and Wyatt's, a bike rental shop, and explore the free-spirited island's rocky coastline.

RIGHT The Portland Head Lighthouse, south of the city in Cape Elizabeth, is postcard Maine.

5 *Free Island* 10 a.m.

The free spirit of **Peaks Island**, part of the archipelago that surrounds Portland, is evident the moment you step off the ferry. If no one is manning **Brad and Wyatt's** (115 Island Avenue; 207-766-5631), a bike rental place housed in a dusty shack, drop some money into the honor-system box ($5 an hour). Then cruise the rocky coastline for the stuff of Maine legend: gorgeous lighthouses, osprey swooping off the surf. The island is pleasantly free of McMansions and private beaches. No wonder the natives tried (unsuccessfully) to secede from Portland a few years back.

6 *Marketing* Noon

A collective moan could be heard when the Public Market, a hangar-size hall run by Maine farmers and fishermen, shuttered in 2006. Luckily, some of those same vendors pooled their resources and opened a scaled-back version on Monument Square. Occupying a building from the mid-1800s, the **Public Market House** (28 Monument Square; 207-228-2056; publicmarkethouse.com) is stocked with bread, cheeses, Maine produce, and micro-beer. More recently it expanded into a loft filled with secondhand couches and food stalls, including **Peanut Butter Jelly Time** (207-712-2408; pbjtime.net), which serves variations of one thing, and **Kamasouptra** (207-415-6692; kamasouptra.com), which makes hearty soups like grilled cheese and tomato.

7 *Vintage Maine* 2 p.m.

Search out the most adventurous shops in the maze of stores lining the Old Port, the historic warehouse district. **Madgirl World** (275 Commercial Street; 207-322-3900; madgirlworld.com) is a quirky studio where Meredith Alex recycles skateboards and Barbie dolls into jewelry and funky, eco-friendly dresses; the restroom doubles as a space for monthly art installations. **Ferdinand's** (243 Congress Street; 207-761-2151; ferdinandhomestore.com) carries handmade goods, vintage fashions, novelty cards, and jewelry. When the Old Port palls, drive to Munjoy Hill, a traditional working-class Irish district that now looks more like Notting Hill, with a grassy promenade that overlooks the water. Among its sophisticated establishments are **Rosemont Market & Bakery** (88 Congress Street; 207-773-7888; rosemontmarket.com), which sells fresh breads and sandwiches, and **Angela Adams** (273 Congress Street; 207-774-3523; angelaadams.com), a design store that sells perky home furnishings.

8 *Divine Dining* 8 p.m.

Anchovy truffle butter? The foodie scene is old news here. The latest in Portland's dining scene is reclaimed architecture. A rundown gas station was converted into **El Rayo Taqueria** (101 York Street; 207-780-8226; elrayotaqueria.com), a Mexican cafe with yellow picnic tables. And the old Portland

Savings Bank became **Sonny's** (83 Exchange Street; 207-772-7774; sonnysportland.com; $$), a Latin-themed restaurant. A fine example of this culinary invasion is **Grace** (15 Chestnut Street; 207-828-4422; restaurantgrace.com), a New American restaurant in an 1850s Gothic Revival-style church. There is something divine about drinking next to the nave, or gorging on goat cheese gnocchi surrounded by stained-glass windows.

9 *Bowl for Kicks* 10 p.m.

The bars along Wharf Street can get pretty fratty. For a more memorable evening, roll across town to **Bayside Bowl** (58 Alder Street; 207-791-2695; baysidebowl.com), a 12-lane bowling alley. Even if bowling isn't your thing, you can knock back a few pints of Shipyard ale at the sleek bar, which draws a mostly young crowd with tattoos and tie-dyed shirts. Or skip the bowling entirely and go to **Novare Res** (4 Canal Plaza; 207-761-2437; novareresbiercafe.com), a festive beer garden with long beechwood tables and more than 300 beers that feels more Munich than Maine.

SUNDAY

10 *The Mail Run* 10 a.m.

Schooner tours and lobster boat rides can be touristy, not to mention pricey. A better way to cruise

around scenic Casco Bay is the mail ferry — a courier fleet that hops around five of the islands. The ferry is run by **Casco Bay Lines** (56 Commercial Street; 207-774-7871; cascobaylines.com) and departs twice a day, seven days a week, from the main ferry terminal.

OPPOSITE The fare is Maine Mexican at El Reyo Taqueria, which operates in a repurposed former gas station. Outdoor dining is a summer option.

ABOVE Scratch Baking Co. in South Portland sells oven-fresh breads, muffins, and pizzas.

BELOW A fishing boat in the Portland harbor. Maine seafood and local produce appear on city restaurant menus.

The loop, which costs less than $20, takes three hours, so pack a lunch.

11 *Fermented Fun* 2 p.m.

Mead, or fermented honey, may have gone out of fashion in, oh, the 16th century, but the **Maine Mead Works** (51 Washington Avenue; 207-773-6323; mainemeadworks.com) is bringing it back. The honey winery opened in 2008 in a gritty warehouse on the edge of town and resembles a mad chemist's garage with tanks and tubes everywhere. A few blocks away but in a similar spirit is the **Urban Farm Fermentory** (200 Anderson Street, Bay 4; 207-653-7406; urbanfarmfermentory.com), a producer of cider, sauerkraut, and other fermented comestibles that offers seminars on topics like pickling and eco-friendly mulching. It's another example of how Portland can't seem to get enough of recycling.

ABOVE Imported and domestic cheeses for sale at the Public Market House, a magnet for locavore shoppers on Monument Square.

OPPOSITE The Munjoy Hill neighborhood as seen from the ferry ride to Peaks Island.

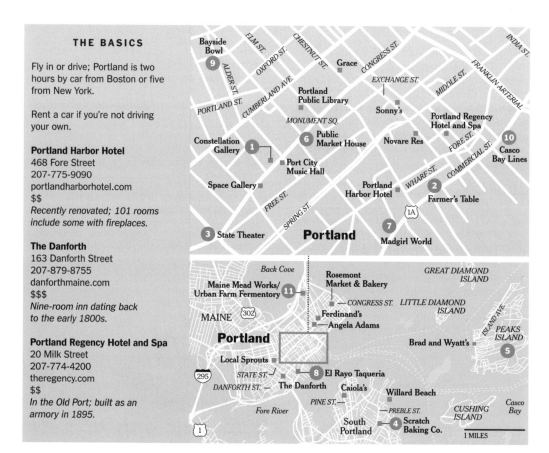

THE BASICS

Fly in or drive; Portland is two hours by car from Boston or five from New York.

Rent a car if you're not driving your own.

Portland Harbor Hotel
468 Fore Street
207-775-9090
portlandharborhotel.com
$$
Recently renovated; 101 rooms include some with fireplaces.

The Danforth
163 Danforth Street
207-879-8755
danforthmaine.com
$$$
Nine-room inn dating back to the early 1800s.

Portland Regency Hotel and Spa
20 Milk Street
207-774-4200
theregency.com
$$
In the Old Port; built as an armory in 1895.

Bar Harbor

Formerly named Eden, Bar Harbor, Maine, may well be the perfect New England tourist town. There are the requisite T-shirt emporiums and fudge shops and homemade-ice cream joints. There are art galleries and chamber music. The architecture consists mainly of grand "cottages" built in the early 20th century by titans of pre-income-tax industry, but they are not about Newportesque excess as much as bygone elegance. Above all else, though, Bar Harbor is special because a few of those early visitors donated their land and pulled the strings to get 40 percent of the incomparably dramatic and beautiful Mount Desert Island, on which Bar Harbor sits, designated as Acadia National Park. Bike, hike, amble, kayak, rock climb, horseback ride, lobster tour, whatever — it's a day tripper's paradise, at least until the leaf peeping ends and the shutters go up around the second week of October.

— BY PAUL SCHNEIDER

FRIDAY

1 *Flickerlight Dining* 8 p.m.

No matter where you're coming from, Bar Harbor is always a little farther away than you estimated. When at last you roll into town, all you really want to do is kick back in an overstuffed chair and eat fresh-baked pizza off a vintage TV table while watching that big hit from Sundance that you missed when it played at home. At **Reel Pizza Cinerama** (33 Kennebec Place; 207-288-3811; reelpizza.net; $$), place your order in the lobby where in a normal movie theater you would be buying popcorn and Junior Mints, and then go into the screening room and stake out a La-Z-Boy. When your number comes up on the screen on the wall, no one minds as you sneak out for your Casino Royale pizza (artichoke hearts, sun-dried tomatoes, and roasted garlic) and another beer.

SATURDAY

2 *Into Wet Air (or Not)* 5 a.m.

Given its extreme eastern location, 1,532-foot **Cadillac Mountain** is said to be the first place in the United States to see the sun rise. But beware, the best-intentioned plans to climb up and greet the dawn may fall victim to classic Maine mist and fog. If so, sleep in until 8 or so and then pick up

a newspaper and wander into **2 Cats** (27 Cottage Street; 207-288-3509; 2catsbarharbor.com; $$) for a breakfast burrito or homemade biscuit and a coffee. With the help of caffeine and newsprint, your personal fog will lift. (Warning to the feline-phobic: yes, you'll see them.)

3 *Here's to You, Mr. Rockefeller* Noon

By 1913 John D. Rockefeller Jr. was already feeling a bit crowded out by all the cars running on his family's gasoline, so he began construction of what became 57 miles of carriage roads that are open only to nonmotorized travelers. Like Mr. R., you want to do your part, so rent bikes at **Acadia Bike** (48 Cottage Street; 800-526-8615; acadiabike.com) and pedal merrily for a couple of hours through the mist along the shore of Eagle Lake, over the granite bridges, and between the dreamy mountains.

4 *Spot of Tea* 2 p.m.

Along the exquisite Park Loop Road, park your bike at the **Jordan Pond House**. By this time,

OPPOSITE AND BELOW Acadia National Park, the creation of a group of early-20th-century preservationists and philanthropists who valued the rocky shores and seascapes of Bar Harbor. Fifty square miles of Mount Desert Island, where Bar Harbor is situated, are in the park.

you'll be ready for its steam-filled popovers and tea (207-276-3316; thejordanpondhouse.com; $$; reservations suggested). The popovers arrive one at a time as you eat them at wooden tables out on the lawn, overlooking the pond and the pair of mountains known as the Bubbles. Afterward, find the bus stop and wait for the free bus that will take you and the bike back to Bar Harbor.

5 *Old Culture, New Culture* 4 p.m.

Back in downtown Bar Harbor, the **Abbe Museum** (26 Mount Desert Street; 207-288-3519; abbemuseum.org) looks back to a Mount Desert culture long preceding the arrival of the Rockefellers. Its displays of artifacts and art from the native peoples who once lived here include masterpieces of Wabanaki quillwork, basketry, and clothing that are almost subversively beautiful in this age of mass production and computer-assisted design.

6 *Sox and Ale* 6 p.m.

Maine, as befitting a state that used to be a part of Massachusetts, is part of the Red Sox nation. The mania is palpable at **Little Anthony's** (131 Cottage Street; 207-288-4700; eatatlittleanthonys.com), where the locals gather. Stop for a pitcher of ale and a few innings. If there are Yankee fans in your party, don't let on.

7 *New England Bistro* 8 p.m.

The locavore sensibility has arrived in Bar Harbor, though it may take looking beyond the obvious tourist-heavy burger joints to find it. At cozy **Mache Bistro** (135 Cottage Street; 207-288-0447; machebistro.com; $$), the owner and chef, Kyle Yarborough, uses ingredients supplied by local farms

and fishermen to create his Maine take on casual French fare. Menus change very frequently, but might include lamb chops and sausage over garlic mashed potatoes or duck breast cassoulet.

SUNDAY

8 *The Beehive* 7:30 a.m.

After loading up on coffee and bagels at **Randonnée Café** (37 Cottage Street, 207-288-9592; randonneecafe.com), drive along Park Loop Road to the Sand Beach parking lot and hike the trail up **Beehive Mountain**. The route is nearly straight up at times, an ascent made possible only by the iron rungs and handrails maintained by the National Park Service. It's not for the faint of heart, but it's short, and on a clear morning you have staggering views out over all the little inlets and islets to yourself. On the way back, take the trail over Gorham Mountain and along the base of the Cadillac Cliffs. It will put you back out on the coast not far from the Thunder Hole, where the air roars its disapproval at being compressed into a cave by the waves. From there

it's an easy walk back to the car and a dip, if you're extremely warm-blooded, at Sand Beach.

9 *Into the Blue* Noon

As you head back to town on the Park Loop Road, stop at the turnoff for Cadillac Mountain and drive up to the summit. Its 360-degree view is more than worth the detour, even if, as is likely, you discover that hundreds of other people feel the same way at exactly the same time.

10 *Put On Your Bib* 1:30 p.m.

As you leave town on Route 3, the time has come at last for lobster. You've turned down all manner of creative crustacean so far ("Uh, what kind of cheese did you say was on that?") because the best way to eat a lobster is with a bib and a cob and a blob of cole slaw. Skip the first lobster pound and any that have tinted-window tour buses parked out front. You could do a lot worse than to get all the way to the **Trenton Bridge Lobster Pound** (1237 Bar Harbor Road; 207-667-2977; trentonbridgelobster.com), just over the bridge in Trenton. After half a century in business, they know how to boil a spider.

OPPOSITE ABOVE A group of kayakers takes a break in a cove on Mount Desert Island's coastline.

OPPOSITE BELOW The Abbe Museum in downtown Bar Harbor.

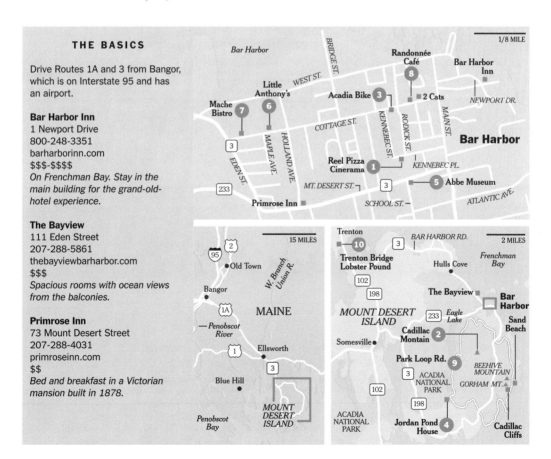

THE BASICS

Drive Routes 1A and 3 from Bangor, which is on Interstate 95 and has an airport.

Bar Harbor Inn
1 Newport Drive
800-248-3351
barharborinn.com
$$$-$$$$
On Frenchman Bay. Stay in the main building for the grand-old-hotel experience.

The Bayview
111 Eden Street
207-288-5861
thebayviewbarharbor.com
$$$
Spacious rooms with ocean views from the balconies.

Primrose Inn
73 Mount Desert Street
207-288-4031
primroseinn.com
$$
Bed and breakfast in a Victorian mansion built in 1878.

Stowe

Envision the idyllic Vermont village: soaring church steeple, covered bridges, no chain stores in sight. That's Stowe, the grande dame of Green Mountain ski towns — which makes it all the more shocking that the ski resort is owned by AIG, the insurance behemoth. That connection helps explain Stowe's $400 million upgrade, with a shiny gondola and a new pedestrian village with a private club and outdoor fire pits galore. But beneath all the modern glitz, Stowe still feels like a quaint place where no one locks the door and folks still dress like Bob Newhart without a hint of irony.
— BY LIONEL BEEHNER

FRIDAY

1 *Maple Flavors* 3 p.m.

On the way into town, stock up on homemade jam from the **Cold Hollow Cider Mill** (3600 Waterbury-Stowe Road; 802-244-8771; coldhollow.com), a farmhouse store that smells like the inside of an 11,000-gallon vat of cider, which just happens to sit in the back. Turn the spigot and help yourself. It goes nicely with the sinfully sweet doughnuts made fresh up front. More provisions wait down the road: the **Cabot Annex Store** (2657 Waterbury-Stowe Road; 802-244-6334) has a smorgasbord of Cheddars — chipotle, horseradish, Tuscan — to sample free.

2 *Old-Time Main Street* 4:30 p.m.

Stroll up Main Street, as folksy as a yellowed New England postcard, past arts-and-crafts shops and century-old inns. **Lackey's** (109 Main Street; 802-253-7624) is an old-fashioned variety store from the mid-1800s with the original wood floor. Or drop by **Shaw's General Store** (54 Main Street; 802-253-4040; heshaw.com) to pick up a rabbit-fur hat or an Icelandic wool sweater. The store dates from the 1890s and still shows off its original wood and tin ceiling.

3 *Vermont Microbrews* 8 p.m.

For good grub at decent prices, head to the **Shed** (1859 Mountain Road; 802-253-4765; $), a casual spot

OPPOSITE The lobby of the new Stowe Mountain Lodge at Spruce Peak.

RIGHT McCarthy's, a popular spot for breakfast.

where shaggy-bearded locals like to name-drop trails over pints of microbrew. The décor is a bit predictable — bumper stickers on the ceiling, deer heads adorned with boas and Mardi Gras beads — but the menu is satisfying, with tasty cheeseburgers and large Cobb salads.

SATURDAY

4 *Irish Send-off* 7 a.m.

Kick off your day at **McCarthy's** (454 Mountain Road; 802-253-8626; $$), a Mel's Diner-like spot where chatty waitresses wink at regulars and out-of-towners alike. Carb-loaded dishes like corned-beef hash, maple-glazed bacon, and honey oatmeal toast draw a packed house. Arrive before 8 a.m. to beat the rush.

5 *Eats, Chutes, and Needles* 8:30 a.m.

Start at **Spruce Peak**'s new base lodge, which has convenient combo lockers, ample parking, and a roomy interior encased in woven timber, before hopping on the still-shiny Over Easy gondola to **Mount Mansfield**. Take another gondola to reach the top, which incidentally is the highest point in Vermont, and feast your eyes on 2,360 vertical feet of powdery terrain. Start off on Gondolier, one of the mountain's signature cruisers with a million well-groomed twists. Once your legs get warmed up, follow the speed demons over to Nosedive, a steep chute that is among the oldest trails in Vermont. For

tree skiing, head to Hayride, a gently sloped glade run with evenly spaced spruces.

6 *Waffle House* Noon

Don't expect a cafeteria with chili bowls and frozen pizzas at the top of Mount Mansfield. This is scenic Vermont, so lunch means a casual sit-down at the **Cliff House** (802-253-3665; $$-$$$), a timber lodge with old wooden tables that serves upscale fare. Favorites include Prince Edward Island mussels, rich lamb stew, and daily crepe specials. Soaring floor-to-cathedral-ceiling windows offer sunny views of Smuggler's Notch and Mount Washington on the horizon. Grab a chocolate-coated waffle on your way out.

7 *Stowe's Better Half* 1:30 p.m.

After lunch, follow the sun over to **Spruce Peak**, the smaller of Stowe's two mountains. Once the neglected stepchild of Mount Mansfield and ignored by groomers, Spruce Peak now has great cruiser trails, new snow-making, and a newish quad chair replacing a creaky lift that took 20 minutes to reach the top. Main Street and Sterling are wide-open cruisers with lots of variety. If you find yourself back on Mount Mansfield, a nice and easy chaser to a long day of skiing is Toll Road, a never-ending trail with gorgeous views.

8 *A Secret Trail* 4 p.m.

Stowe has a lively après ski scene, which begins as early as 2 p.m. on weekends and seems more crowded since the resort did away with its night skiing a few years back. Insiders take the Bruce Trail, a cross-country path that winds its way to the **Matterhorn Bar** (4969 Mountain Road; 802-253-8198; matterhornbar.com). Stuffed with pool tables, a disco ball, and waitresses in trucker hats serving Pabst

ABOVE Snowboarding near the summit of Mount Mansfield, the highest point in Vermont.

RIGHT Spruce Peak at Stowe Mountain Resort.

Blue Ribbon, it is a raucous but civilized place to unwind after a day on the slopes. A wooden patio and sushi bar overlooks a brook, while a cover band plays classic rock up front.

9 *Spruced Up* 8 p.m.

The centerpiece of Spruce Peak is the **Stowe Mountain Lodge**, a six-story compound of exposed timber and stonework. Lamps look like twisted logs, and you're never more than 20 feet from a roaring, if gas-fueled, fireplace. Ascend the staircase to **Solstice** (802-760-4735; stowemountainlodge.com; $$-$$$), whose soaring salmon-toned walls, white-stone fireplaces, and open kitchen make it feel like the great room in an outdoorsy billionaire's house. The New American cuisine uses regional ingredients and has included dishes like Maine lobster risotto and Newfoundland steelhead trout.

10 *My Way or the Highway* 10 p.m.

The **Rusty Nail** (1190 Mountain Road; 802-253-6245; rustynailbar.com; $$) looks right out of the 1980s movie *Road House*. Gritty, crowded, with the stench of stale beer and a beefy tattooed bouncer out front, this popular spot serves up microbrews and martinis while live music keeps the crowds swinging on the sunken dance floor. Check out the outdoors ice bar most weekends.

SUNDAY

11 *Vroom with a View* 10 a.m.

To see Stowe's backcountry up close, jump aboard a snowmobile and glide over 10 heart-racing miles of luge-like twists and turns. Expect gorgeous scenery and occasional scowls from cross-country skiers. Two-hour tours are about $150 per person from **Stowe Snowmobile Tours** (849 South Main Street; 802-253-6221; snowmobilevermont.com).

12 *Sugar-Coated Rubdown* Noon

The smell of wood crackling in the two-way fireplace and a plate of homemade cookies greet guests to the **Topnotch Resort and Spa** (4000 Mountain Road; 802-253-8585; topnotchresort.com; spa entry, $50), where the 35,000-square-foot spa and gym was recently renovated. Kick your feet up by the large indoor pool bedecked in blond wood and sip some mint tea. Or soak in the outdoor hot tub overlooking Mount Mansfield. Even better, swaddle yourself in a terry cloth robe, slap on some June Jacobs facial cream, and tuck into a cozy treatment room for a rubdown with a concoction using — what else? — Vermont maple syrup.

ABOVE Inside Stowe Mercantile, one of the appealing spots for browsing and buying on Main Street.

THE BASICS

The Burlington airport is about an hour away. By car, Stowe is about five hours from New York City.

Stowe Mountain Lodge
7412 Mountain Road
802-253-3560
stowemountainlodge.com
$$$$
The only ski-in, ski-out hotel at the mountain. Marble baths, balconies, fireplaces.

Topnotch Resort and Spa
4000 Mountain Road
802-253-8585
topnotchresort.com
$$$$
The best rooms face the slopes, not the parking lot.

Green Mountain Inn
18 Main Street
802-253-7301
greenmountaininn.com
$$
Book a room in the main lodge, built in 1833.

1 MILE

Smuggler's Notch

GREEN MOUNTAINS

7 Spruce Peak

108

Cliff House

6

Over Easy Gondola

5

9 Stowe Mountain Lodge/ Solstice

Mt. Mansfield

VERMONT

MT. MANSFIELD STATE FOREST

8 Matterhorn Bar

12 Topnotch Resort and Spa

WEEKS HILL RD.

108

1/4 MILE

4 McCarthy's Restaurant

Rusty Nail

Shed 3

10

MOUNTAIN RD.

Stowe

Lackey's

2

100

Stowe

MAIN ST.

MAPLE RD.

Green Mountain Inn

Shaw's General Store

100

Stowe Snowmobile Tours 11

Cold Hollow Cider Mill/ Cabot Annex 1

CANADA

Burlington

Area of detail

91

Montpelier

VERMONT

GREEN MOUNTAIN NATIONAL FOREST

89

93

N.Y.

N.H.

40 MILES

Burlington

It is no surprise that Burlington, Vermont, a city whose biggest exports include the jam band Phish and Ben & Jerry's ice cream, has a hip, socially conscious vibe. But in counterpoint to its worldliness—antiglobalization rallies and fair-trade products abound—Burlington turns a discerning eye to the local. The Lake Champlain shoreline has undergone a renaissance, with gleaming new hotels, bike and sailboat rental shops, and parks with sweeping views of the Adirondack Mountains. In the city's restaurants, local means locavore; urbane menus are filled with heirloom tomatoes and grass-fed beef from (where else?) Vermont. And you're practically required to wash it all down with a local microbrew.
— BY KATIE ZEZIMA

FRIDAY

1 *Stroll, Shop, Snack* 4:30 p.m.

With its eclectic mix of students, activists, artists, families, and professors (the University of Vermont is based here), Burlington offers some interesting people-watching. Take in the sights at the **Church Street Marketplace** (2 Church Street; churchstmarketplace.com), a wide, four-block concourse that is the city's social center and home to more than 100 shops and restaurants. The pace is slow, leisurely, and crowded, so be sure to leave plenty of time to explore. Pop into **Sweet Lady Jane** (40 Church Street; 802-862-5051; sweetladyjane.biz) for funky women's clothes and accessories; **Frog Hollow** (85 Church Street; 802-863-6458; froghollow.org) to check out treasures created by Vermont artists; and **Lake Champlain Chocolates** (65 Church Street; 802-862-5185; lakechamplainchocolates.com), where a hot chocolate doubles as a meal and you'll be hard put to eat just one truffle.

2 *Chic Tables* 7:30 p.m.

Long known as a town for gravy fries, pizza, and other collegiate staples, Burlington has seen a flurry of upscale restaurants opening in recent years. **L'Amante** (126 College Street; 802-863-5200; lamante.com; $$$) helped lead the charge. If one were to take Tuscany and add a splash of Vermont, the result would be this hearty yet crunchy menu. Starters might include squash blossom fritters, and main dishes include items like grilled Vermont quail. It's sleek and low-lit, yet somehow informal, despite an expensive wine list that leans heavily on Italian reds.

3 *Music and Maple Syrup* 10 p.m.

If there are three things that Burlington does well, they are live music, beer, and coffee. **Radio Bean** (8 North Winooski Avenue; 802-660-9346; radiobean.com), a coffee bar with exposed brick walls covered in local artworks, has all three. It's like hearing a band at a friend's party, if your friend lives in a ridiculously cool loft. Try the Five Dollar Shake, a brilliant concoction of stout, espresso, and maple syrup that satisfies your desire to drink beer and stay awake at the same time. And yes, it's $5.

SATURDAY

4 *View from a Bicycle* 9 a.m.

Playing outside, whether on ski slopes, hiking trails, or lakes, is a way of life in Burlington, so it's no surprise that biking is a popular way to get around. Rent a bike at one of the many local shops like **North Star Sports** (100 Main Street; 802-863-3832; northstarsportsvt.com), for about $20 an hour or $30 a day. For those who want to see the city, marked bike lanes make it easy to ride, but its steep hills will have your quads thinking otherwise. Head out along Lake Champlain, however, and the terrain is mostly

OPPOSITE A winter view of the Burlington Community Boathouse and Lake Champlain.

RIGHT The Frog Hollow Gift Shop, an arts center and gallery of Vermont-made arts and crafts.

flat, joining to some 1,100 miles of trails crisscrossing through New York and Canada. Maps are available at champlainbikeways.org.

5 *Weightless Suds* 1 p.m.

Chances are **American Flatbread Burlington Hearth** (115 St. Paul Street; 802-861-2999; americanflatbread.com; $) will be packed with everyone from kids to beer geeks when you get there. But don't panic; just order one of the Zero Gravity house beers—this place specializes in Belgian styles. The crispy flatbreads, baked in a wood-fired hearth, are essentially thin-crust pizzas topped with things like kalamata olives, sweet red peppers, goat cheese, rosemary, and red onions.

6 *Wrecks and Monsters* 3 p.m.

Lake Champlain isn't just what makes Burlington so picturesque. It's also a huge ecosystem that is the home of one of the world's oldest coral reefs (now fossilized) and hundreds of species of fish and plants. The **ECHO Lake Aquarium and Science Center** (at the Leahy Center for Lake Champlain, 1 College Street; 877-324-6386; echovermont.org) explores the scientific, ecological, and cultural and historical importance of the lake with hands-on exhibitions, including the remnants of an old shipwreck and an installation that gives visitors new respect for frogs. Children will enjoy working in a recreated paleontologic dig box, and adults will marvel at the lake's complexity. The center even explores Lake Champlain's biggest mystery: Is Champ a mythical lake monster or real? Try to spot him from the second-floor deck.

7 *No Page Unturned* 5 p.m.

Reading and recycling are cultivated arts in Burlington, and no place combines both better than the **Crow Bookshop** (14 Church Street; 802-862-0848; crowbooks.com). Stroll on the creaky wooden floor and browse a trove of used and rare books as well as publishers' overstocks, ranging from gardening guides to gently used copies of Shakespeare. Let

the children explore their part of the store while you hang out on one of the couches and thumb through a stranger's old textbook.

8 *Paris in Vermont* 8 p.m.

In a city where style is inspired more by Birkenstocks than Birkin bags, **Leunig's Bistro** (115 Church Street; 802-863-3759; leunigsbistro.com; $$) offers a welcome dash of French flair. With its cherub lamps, cozy booths, and alfresco dining, it remains a social center. Go for a traditional beef Bourguignon or look for something with a local touch, perhaps maple-and-cardamom-marinated pork loin.

9 *Choose Your Nightlife* 10:30 p.m.

Follow the thumping bass to **Red Square** (136 Church Street; 802-859-8909; redsquarevt.com), a friendly nightclub that draws club kids and music lovers. Live bands usually play the first half of the night or, if the weather permits, on the outdoor patio. Late night is for D.J.'s spinning hip-hop, rock, and reggae to college students in halter tops and T-shirts. For something on the mellower side, head to **Nectar's** (188 Main Street; 802-658-4771; liveatnectars.com), the club where Phish got its start. Not interested in live music? Walk to **Green Room** (86 St. Paul Street; 802-651-9669; greenroomburlington.com) for a nightcap on a cushy sofa.

SUNDAY

10 *Green Eggs or Tofu* 11 a.m.

Prefer tofu in your scramble? Try **Magnolia Bistro** (1 Lawson Lane; 802-846-7446; magnoliabistro.com;

$), where eggs are always interchangeable for tofu and homemade granola is on the menu. For meat eaters, there are choices like an open-faced steak sandwich with Cheddar or tarragon chicken sandwich. Magnolia also claims to be one of Burlington's most environmentally friendly restaurants, which means it must be really, really green. Indeed, everything is recycled, and it's certified by the national Green Restaurant Association.

11 *Could This Be Stonehenge?* 1 p.m.

Not sure of the time? Find out at the **Burlington Earth Clock**, a 43-foot-wide sundial at **Oakledge Park and Beach** (end of Flynn Street) made of slabs of granite from local quarries. Stand in the middle and look toward the mountains; the stones in front of you represent where the sun sets during equinoxes and

solstices. Also in the park is a studio-size treehouse reachable even for kids in wheelchairs. It's an inclusive childhood fantasy come true.

OPPOSITE ABOVE On the popular Burlington Bike Path.

OPPOSITE BELOW The Earth Clock, a 42-foot sundial, shares Oakledge Park with a swimming beach, picnic and recreation spaces, and a wheelchair-accessible treehouse.

ABOVE Church Street Marketplace, the place for shopping, people watching, and decadent hot chocolate.

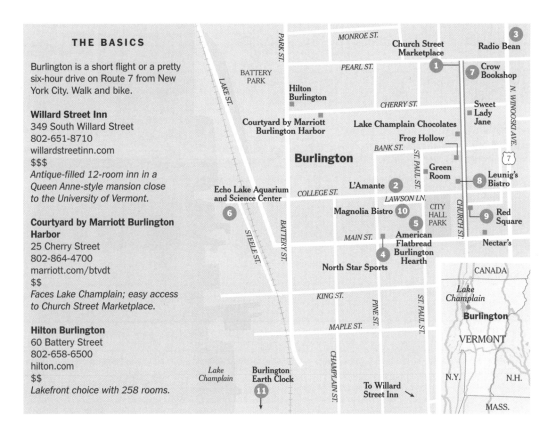

THE BASICS

Burlington is a short flight or a pretty six-hour drive on Route 7 from New York City. Walk and bike.

Willard Street Inn
349 South Willard Street
802-651-8710
willardstreetinn.com
$$$
Antique-filled 12-room inn in a Queen Anne-style mansion close to the University of Vermont.

Courtyard by Marriott Burlington Harbor
25 Cherry Street
802-864-4700
marriott.com/btvdt
$$
Faces Lake Champlain; easy access to Church Street Marketplace.

Hilton Burlington
60 Battery Street
802-658-6500
hilton.com
$$
Lakefront choice with 258 rooms.

Lake Placid

In any trip to Lake Placid, there will be a moment when you catch yourself thinking: Do you believe this little place was the host of two Olympic Games? Not because something so symbolic and global does not fit in a tiny upstate New York village of 3,000, but, more striking, because it will dawn on you that it is the perfect place. While the Olympics have become outsized, intimate Lake Placid retains ties to simpler times, whether 1932, when the Winter Games first came to visit, or 1980, a time remembered fondly by Americans for the Miracle-on-Ice United States hockey team. Still, a visit is less about the Olympics as they were than about life as it was. Lake Placid has the rhythm of a small town, albeit one with the sophistication to have played host to the world, and its pace is spiked by active people who embrace the mountain and lake setting that has attracted visitors for centuries. In the end, at least occasionally, you have to buy into the Olympic motto — Swifter, Higher, Stronger — and just go with it. Oh, and hold on for dear life. — BY BILL PENNINGTON

FRIDAY

1 *A Reason to Scream* 7 p.m.

Park your car in the center of the village, get out and follow the screaming. It will lead you to a three-story ramp next to Mirror Lake. You're here in winter, so buy a ticket to rent a toboggan. (Don't look up.) Climb to the top of this converted ski jump and place your toboggan on the solid-ice runway. (Don't look down.) Someone will push you down the steep chute, and after a few harrowing seconds at 40 miles an hour, you will be flung out across the frozen lake. (Don't get out.) The toboggan often does 360-degree turns before it stops. Then get up and do it again. (Don't forget to scream this time.) You have just experienced the **Lake Placid Toboggan Chute** (Parkside Drive; 518-523-2591; northelba.org/government/park-district/toboggan-chute.html).

OPPOSITE Mirror Lake in Lake Placid on a fall day, before the Adirondack snowfalls and the winter rush.

RIGHT Snow-season downtime in one of the cozy common rooms at the Mirror Lake Inn.

2 *Toast Your Triumph* 8 p.m.

Now that you have been baptized in the ways of the Olympic village, your bravery will be rewarded at the **Lake Placid Pub and Brewery** (813 Mirror Lake Drive; 518-523-3813; lakeplacidpubandbrewery.com), a few steps from the toboggan chute. Its signature Ubu Ale, a dark, smooth brew, will quickly calm your nerves.

3 *Window or Hearth?* 9 p.m.

A short trip up the hill overlooking the village of Lake Placid, on Olympic Drive, is a wonderful way to get the lay of the land, even at night. That frozen patch where your toboggan flew, Mirror Lake, is the dominant feature of the village. (Lake Placid itself is to the north.) This view of the village is best from **Veranda** (1 Olympic Drive; 518-523-3339; lakeplacidcp.com/dining.htm; $$$), where you can warm up at a table by the fire or look out from a table with lake and mountain views. This is the Adirondacks, so order the duck.

SATURDAY

4 *Expanded Slopes* 9 a.m.

Although *Ski Magazine* has called **Whiteface Mountain**, about seven miles from Lake Placid, the best ski area in the Eastern United States, somehow the place remains perhaps the most underrated snow sports destination in North America. People used to say it was too hard and too cold. It is true Whiteface's black diamond runs include the steep trails used

for the 1980 Olympic races, but the mountain has expanded its terrain to soften the harsh edges. There is something good for everyone now at Whiteface, most of all, a speedy—and warm—gondola.

5 *A Bite at the Brown Dog* 2 p.m.

With few lift lines at Whiteface it is easy to pack a whole day's skiing into a few hours, so don't be surprised when you find yourself back in the village in time for a late lunch. The **Brown Dog Cafe and**

Wine Bar (2409 Main Street; 518-523-3036; $$) has sandwiches and salads as well as a selection of red and white wines. It also has a view of Mirror Lake—look, there goes another toboggan.

6 *Where'd You Get That Hat?* 3 p.m.

Lake Placid's Main Street is a door-to-door feast of shops featuring Adirondack-style furniture and outdoor-inspired clothing. Be sure to poke your head into **Where'd You Get That Hat?** (2569 Main Street; 518-523-3101; wheredyougetthathat.com). When you make a purchase of this store's distinctive headgear, and you will, it is guaranteed that people will approach you for the next several months to ask, "Where'd you get that hat?" The appropriate response: "Exactly." Before leaving Main Street, duck into the **Olympic Center** (2634 Main Street; 518-523-1655; whiteface.com/facilities/oc.php), home to the Miracle on Ice hockey rink from 1980. You may be stunned by how small it is. An Olympic museum at the same address has an exhibit devoted to the 1980 team, as well as skating outfits and pink skates from Sonja Henie, the figure-skating darling of the 1932 Olympics.

ABOVE The Olympic speed skating oval, where Eric Heiden won five gold medals in the 1980 Winter Games, is open to the public for skating.

LEFT Whiteface Mountain, where Olympic skiers raced.

7 *Spa Treatment* 5 p.m.

You could rent skates and push yourself around the 400-meter oval where Eric Heiden won his five gold medals, but come on, enough is enough. It's time to pamper those tense toboggan muscles and stretched skiing tendons at the **Spa at the Mirror Lake Inn** (77 Mirror Lake Drive; 518-302-3010; mirrorlakeinn.com). Tranquillity reigns in this sanctuary. Besides, it's really nice to stop and plop into the hot tub.

8 *Critters by Candlelight* 7 p.m.

Stay at the Mirror Lake Inn and take a table at the **View** (518-302-3000; $$$), its tablecloth-and-candlelight restaurant. An eclectic menu ranges to dishes like rutabaga-and-mushroom tournedos, but again, this is winter in the Adirondacks, and you really ought to order game. There's usually some on the menu, perhaps quail or grilled rack of wild boar. If not, you can always make do with the beef.

SUNDAY

9 *Do You Iditarod?* 10 a.m.

Alaska is not the only place to go dog-sledding. Just off Main Street, **Thunder Mountain Dog Sled Tours** (518-891-6239; across from the High Peaks Resort) will have you mushing around Mirror Lake in no time. Watch out for flying toboggans.

10 *Lakefront Lunch* 11 a.m.

A few miles outside the village is the **Lake Placid Lodge** (144 Lodge Way; 518-523-2700; lakeplacidlodge.com), a place both refined and rustic. It is also a place of fine dining. In **Maggie's**

TOP Dogsledding on frozen Mirror Lake.

ABOVE The view from the top of the Lake Placid bobsled run, which was used in the 1932 and 1980 Olympics.

Pub ($$$$), even the burgers on the lunch menu have suggested wine pairings.

11 *Bobsled Finale* 1 p.m.

Now that you are comfortably at ease, it is time to create a lasting memory of Lake Placid. On your way out of town on Route 73, stop at the **Olympic Sports Complex** (220 Bobsled Run Lane; 518-523-4436; whiteface.com/activities/bob.php). Rent a thick, heavy helmet and hire a clear-eyed professional driver and a brakeman who will steer you down the Olympic

bobsled course at 50 or 60 miles an hour. There is much less screaming than at the toboggan run. That may be because you are often sideways or more or less upside down, which for a few seconds turns breathing into a new Olympic sport. All in all, a fitting conclusion to a breathtaking visit.

ABOVE Professional sledders swoosh paying thrill-seekers down the Olympic bobsled run.

OPPOSITE The Follies trail on Whiteface Mountain.

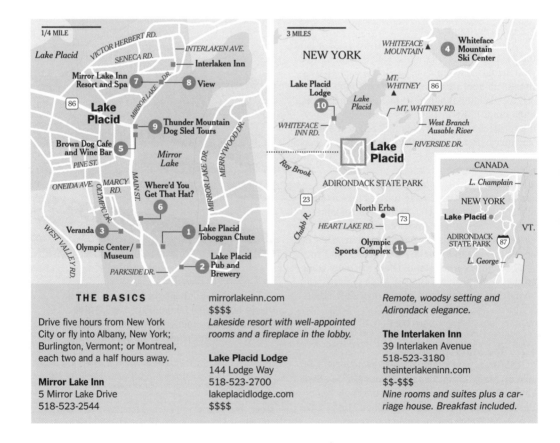

THE BASICS

Drive five hours from New York City or fly into Albany, New York; Burlington, Vermont; or Montreal, each two and a half hours away.

Mirror Lake Inn
5 Mirror Lake Drive
518-523-2544

mirrorlakeinn.com
$$$$
Lakeside resort with well-appointed rooms and a fireplace in the lobby.

Lake Placid Lodge
144 Lodge Way
518-523-2700
lakeplacidlodge.com
$$$$

Remote, woodsy setting and Adirondack elegance.

The Interlaken Inn
39 Interlaken Avenue
518-523-3180
theinterlakeninn.com
$$-$$$
Nine rooms and suites plus a carriage house. Breakfast included.

Cooperstown

High culture or sports worship? In Cooperstown, New York, a dilettante's delight of a tree-shaded Victorian town, you can indulge in both. Many of the half-million or so visitors who come each year are bent only on seeing the National Baseball Hall of Fame. But another sizable crowd arrives for the well-regarded Glimmerglass Opera, also an established part of the summer season. And long before anyone had heard of A-Rod or even Babe Ruth, Cooperstown was a pilgrimage site as the home of James Fenimore Cooper, the early-19th-century superstar author whose wildly popular novels, including The Deerslayer *and* The Last of the Mohicans, *put a haze of romance on an upstate New York frontier that had already vanished. So pack your baseball cap and your opera glasses, and come prepared to celebrate your versatility.*

— BY JOHN MOTYKA

FRIDAY

1 *Abner Shopped Here* 4 p.m.

No matter which team you deify, **Main Street**'s shops will provide jerseys, mugs, engraved bats, and logo-imprinted bath rugs. If you also collect baseball cards, you're in heaven. Abner Doubleday, once known as the father of baseball, trod the streets of this preserved downtown before his days as a Civil War general. His baseball connection was eventually exposed as a myth, but by then Cooperstown had become a baseball shrine in its own right. Nearby on Fair Street is a statue of James Fenimore Cooper in Cooper Park, an unlikely oasis of quiet behind the Baseball Hall of Fame.

2 *Get a Glimmer* 6 p.m.

Wander down to **Lakefront Park** for a good look at Lake Otsego, the deep glacial lake that appeared in Cooper's novels as Glimmerglass. He described it as "a broad sheet of water, so placid and limpid that it resembled a bed of pure mountain atmosphere compressed into a setting of hills and woods."

OPPOSITE Collectibles in a Cooperstown shop. Main Street retailers aim to satisfy the baseball fan.

RIGHT The Farmers' Museum, a working replica of 1800s rural life in upstate New York.

Warriors concealed themselves in those woods, and in *The Deerslayer*, an eccentric frontiersman lived on a primitive houseboat on the lake with his spirited daughters. It's less dramatic today, but the park is a good place to sit and watch sailboats drift by.

3 *Take Your Table* 7 p.m.

Back on Main Street, settle in for drinks and dinner at **Alex & Ika** (149 Main Street; 607-547-4070; $$$). The street scene outside may be reminiscent of Fan Day at the stadium, but the food inside is several cuts above the ballpark hot dog. Look for dishes like a star anise confit of duck with lemon grass kaffir-leaf coconut curry.

SATURDAY

4 *Start with Art* 10 a.m.

The neo-Georgian mansion that is now the **Fenimore Art Museum** (5798 State Route 80; 607-547-1400; about $30 for a combination ticket that will also cover your afternoon stops) occupies the former site of James Fenimore Cooper's farmhouse and displays family artifacts including fan mail from the Marquis de Lafayette (Cooper's books quickly made a splash in Europe and by now have been translated into 40 languages). Downstairs is the Thaw Collection of American Indian Art. Exhibits have

included 20th-century Magnum news photography and John Singer Sargent portraits of women.

5 *Literary Perspectives* 11:30 a.m.

From the museum windows, look out at Cooper's view of the lake and imagine him mentally populating its shores with the crack shot Natty Bumppo (the Deerslayer); Natty's Mohican friend Chingachgook and Chingachgook's wife-to-be, Hist; and the Indian enemies who would capture Hist, requiring her rescue. Then, at the museum shop, pick up a copy of *Rural Hours*, by the author's daughter, Susan Fenimore Cooper. This natural history classic, published in 1850, won her belated recognition as America's first great woman nature writer. It preceded *Walden* by four years, and Thoreau referred to it in his journal.

6 *Farm Yes, Factory No* Noon

Drive across the road to the **Farmers' Museum** (5775 Route 80; 607-547-1450; farmersmuseum.org), 29 buildings that function as a working replica of an 1800s farm and town. In the unlikely event that you've never seen a restored village, you may want to return for a full day; otherwise, pick up lunch at one of the cafes and have a quick look around at the cows and chickens, the schoolhouse, and the work of the artisans on staff. The packets for the museum's heirloom seeds are printed on a treadle press. Outside, children ride wooden farm animals on a carousel.

7 *Out with the Crowd* 2 p.m.

You don't have to be a diehard fan to have a good time at the **National Baseball Hall of Fame** (25 Main Street; 888-425-563-3263; baseballhall.org), but memories of childhood days at the ballpark

with Dad, or your own starring role in Little League, will only make it better. The well-presented exhibits take you on a journey from the game's early origins to the current season, and the oak-lined Hall of Fame Gallery honors baseball's greats, from the first five elected in 1936 to the present. See Yogi Berra's catcher's mitt, Hank Aaron's locker, and mementoes of the old Negro League. And that's just the beginning.

8 *Dinner before the Show* 6 p.m.

It's all about the view at the **Blue Mingo Grill**, situated just a couple of miles northwest of town (Sam Smith's Boatyard, 6098 State Highway 80; 607-547-7496; bluemingogrill.com; $$), so reserve a table as close to the lakefront windows as you can. The lemon-grass-marinated lamb or corn-crusted

ABOVE Otsego Lake, the inspiration for the Glimmerglass of James Fenimore Cooper's *The Deerslayer*.

BELOW Shopping for souvenirs on Main Street, near the Baseball Hall of Fame.

shrimp with hot and sweet onions will be perfectly decent, but your principal mission here is to watch the ripples and mellow out before the show. You're on your way to the opera.

9 *High Notes* 8 p.m.

The **Glimmerglass Opera** (7300 Route 80; 607-547-2255; glimmerglass.org), in its striking 900-seat Alice Busch Opera Theater, draws a sophisticated clientele and has a well-earned reputation for quality and variety. Past summer programs have included an American premiere of Handel's *Tolomeo*; a grouping of operas adapted from Shakespeare with the Cole Porter musical *Kiss Me, Kate*, and four operatic takes on the Orpheus story. Every season also includes standard audience-pleasing fare from the likes of Verdi, Puccini, and Rossini. If you arrive early, you'll find a campus of 43 lakeside acres to stroll on.

SUNDAY

10 *Make a Commitment* 10 a.m.

It's time to decide who you really are. Option One: Check for amateur games and take a look around at quaint **Doubleday Field** (Main Street; 607-547-2270), a 9,000-seat stadium. Then go next door to Doubleday Batting Range and while away the morning testing yourself against the same kind of pitching machine used in major-league training. Option Two: Keep stimulating that literary imagination with a drive a few miles north to **Glimmerglass State Park** (1527 Route 31). Just up the hill from the parking lot for Hyde Hall, a 19th-century mansion, find the trail on Mount Wellington and plunge into the woods. You won't see Hist or Susan Cooper, but they'd both be right at home amid the birches and hemlocks.

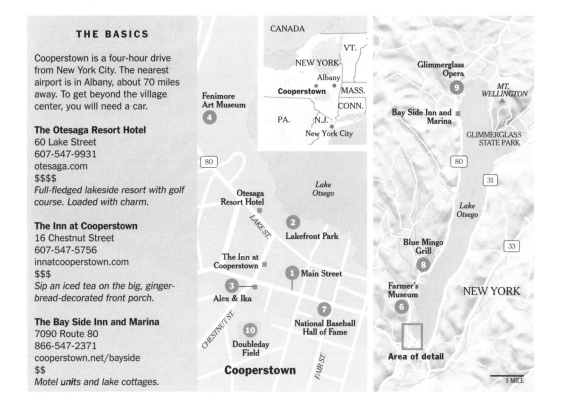

THE BASICS

Cooperstown is a four-hour drive from New York City. The nearest airport is in Albany, about 70 miles away. To get beyond the village center, you will need a car.

The Otesaga Resort Hotel
60 Lake Street
607-547-9931
otesaga.com
$$$$
Full-fledged lakeside resort with golf course. Loaded with charm.

The Inn at Cooperstown
16 Chestnut Street
607-547-5756
innatcooperstown.com
$$$
Sip an iced tea on the big, ginger-bread-decorated front porch.

The Bay Side Inn and Marina
7090 Route 80
866-547-2371
cooperstown.net/bayside
$$
Motel units and lake cottages.

Montreal

French or English? One of the beautiful things about Montreal is that you never know in what language you will be greeted. Which brings up a second thing: Maybe it's the good food, the open skies, or the free-spirited students who call this city their campus, but the folks of Montreal are friendly. Ask someone for directions in the Métro, part of the vast Underground City that stays toasty during the winter, and you may end up making drinks plans later. That's not a bad thing, bien sûr. With the city's music-charged night life, slaughterhouse-chic restaurants, and postindustrial revival, it helps to have a guide. — BY DENNY LEE

FRIDAY

1 *Get Wheels* 4:30 p.m.

Public bikes have swept Europe, so leave it to Montreal, "the other Paris," to popularize the concept in North America. When 5,000 gray-and-red Bixi bikes were deployed in 2009, they became an instant hit. Familiarize yourself with the system: it's as easy as swiping a credit card at one of the 400 **Bixi** stations and going for a spin. (Go to bixi.com for details.) It's one of the quickest ways to get around and, at 5 Canadian dollars (about the same in U.S. dollars) for 24 hours, among the cheapest. To find the nearest Bixi station, including a large one on Rue McGill with 20 docks, download one of the many iPhone apps that offer real-time updates on available bikes, including Bixou Lite (free).

2 *Downtown Roll* 5 p.m.

A bike is only as good as the network it's on. And Montreal delivers, with 310-plus miles of bike lanes that crisscross the city, about half of which are physically separated from cars. To see why Montreal was designated a Unesco City of Design in 2006, point your handlebars toward the Lachine Canal, a former industrial waterfront that has been transformed into a lush green belt. The path is dotted with architectural gems like **Habitat 67** (2600, avenue Pierre-Dupuy; habitat67.com), a Brutalist-style experiment in

modular housing designed by Moshe Safdie. Or pedal along Boulevard de Maisonneuve, which cuts through downtown Montreal, where a 2.1-mile path is named after the late Claire Morissette, a cycling activist.

3 *Québécois Plates* 8 p.m.

Normand Laprise, who pioneered the use of fresh Québécois ingredients at the pricey Toqué!, often praised by critics as the city's best restaurant, opened a midpriced sister restaurant in 2010, **Brasserie t!** (1425, rue Jeanne Mance; 514-282-0808; brasserie-t.com; $$$). Situated at the foot of the Contemporary Art Museum, the brasserie looks like a sleek cargo container. Inside, a contemporary French menu showcases unfussy dishes like grilled flank steak and cod brandade.

4 *Musical Mile* 10 p.m.

The music snobs may have moved on, but it's still impossible to talk about the Mile End district without name-dropping bands like Arcade Fire and the gritty stages that gave them their start. The beloved Green Room closed because of a fire, but upstart bands are still jamming at **Divan Orange** (4234, boulevard St.-Laurent; 514-840-9090; divanorange.org). An alternative, with a bigger stage and sound, is **Il Motore** (179, rue Jean-Talon Ouest; 514-284-0122; ilmotore.ca). To see who's playing, pick up either of the two free art weeklies, *Hour* or *Mirror*.

SATURDAY

5 *Like the Marais* 10 a.m.

While Mile End is still the place to hear bands, its retail scene has cooled off. The action has shifted to

OPPOSITE The Biosphere, designed by Buckminster Fuller for an exposition in 1967, lives on as a Montreal landmark.

RIGHT Bixi bikes, cheap to rent and ride around town.

Old Montreal, where historic cobblestones and high foot traffic ensure the survival of indie boutiques. For homegrown designers like Denis Gagnon and Arielle de Pinto, squeeze inside **Reborn** (231, rue St.-Paul Ouest, Suite 100; 514-499-8549; reborn.ws), a small shop with a sharp eye. Down the block is **À Table Tout le Monde** (361, rue St.-Paul Ouest; 514-750-0311; atabletoutlemonde.com), an elegant store that carries

ABOVE Get a glimpse of Moshe Safdie's Habitat 67, an experiment in modular housing, from the Lachine Canal bike path.

BELOW The path along the Lachine Canal is part of a 300-mile system of bicycle routes and lanes in Montreal.

exquisitely crafted ceramics and housewares. And while you're exploring the historic district, drop into **DHC Art** (451, rue St.-Jean; 514-849-3742; dhc-art.org), one of the city's leading contemporary art galleries.

6 *Three Little Pigs* 1 p.m.
Blame it on the poutine and foie gras, but Montreal was early to the nose-to-tail game, with countless meat-centric restaurants around town. But how many can also claim their own organic garden out back? That's one of the surprises at **McKiernan** (2485, rue Notre-Dame Ouest; 514-759-6677; mckiernanbaravin.com: $$), the latest in a mini-empire of restaurants from the same trio behind the much-hyped Joe Beef and Liverpool House, which are next door. Another surprise? McKiernan might look like a farm-stand luncheonette, with checkered wax paper liners and tin baskets, but the food is top flight. Try the porchetta tacos, made with fresh tortillas.

7 *City of Design* 4 p.m.
An inviting strip of design shops has sprung up along Rue Amherst. One of the smallest is also the nicest, **Montreal Modern** (No. 1853; 514-293-7903; mtlmodern.com), which feels like a midcentury modern jewel box. If you like your modern design on a grander scale, the **Musée des Beaux-Arts de Montreal** (1379-80, rue Sherbrooke Ouest; 514-285-2000; mmfa.qc.ca) has a strong collection, along with Old

Masters and contemporary Canadian artists. And the **Canadian Centre for Architecture** (1920, rue Baile; 514-939-7026; cca.qc.ca) holds regular exhibitions on architecture and urbanism in a striking 19th-century mansion with a modern stone addition.

8 *French Bites* 8 p.m.

A neighborhood wine bar that happens to serve terrific food is one of those pleasures that make Paris, well, Paris. That's the vibe at **Buvette Chez Simone** (4869, avenue du Parc; 514-750-6577; buvettechezsimone.com; $$$), an oaky bar in Mile End with sly design touches. The comfy brasserie

ABOVE The dance floor at the Velvet Speakeasy.

BELOW A Jenny Holzer exhibit at DHC Art, one of the city's leading contemporary art galleries. DHC is part of a trendy retail and art scene in cobblestoned Old Montreal.

menu features dishes like a roast chicken served on a carving board with roasted potatoes. If you're hankering for more inventive fare, bike over to **Pullman** (3424, avenue du Parc; 514-288-7779; pullman-mtl.com; $$$), a high-end tapas bar that serves clever plates like venison tartare, foie gras cookies, and olives with candied lemon. The crowd at both restaurants skews young, fashionable, and chatty.

9 *Electronic Artists* 10 p.m.

In another sign of Euro-flair, techno music is huge in Montreal. And one of the coolest parties is thrown by **Neon** (iloveneon.ca), a digital music collective that has showcased a who's who of electronic artists like

Glass Candy and Hudson Mohawke. Many events take place at **Le Belmont sur le Boulevard** (4483, boulevard St.-Laurent; 514-845-8443; lebelmont.com), an intimate club that has a pool table up front and a pulsing sound system in the rear. For a more analog vibe, head to **Velvet Speakeasy** (420, rue St.-Gabriel; velvetspeakeasy.ca), a posh club in the Old Port district.

SUNDAY

10 *Eggs to Go* 11 a.m.

For a delightful brunch served in an old town house with communal tables, look no farther than **Le Cartet** (106, rue McGill; 514-871-8887; lecartet.com; $$). Part cafe, part grocery store, Le Cartet draws young families and professionals with hearty platters of eggs that come with figs, cheese, and salad greens.

On your way out, feel free to stock up on crusty baguettes, French mustards, and picnic cheeses.

11 *Dancing Man* 2 p.m.

If it's sunny, join Montreal's barefoot and pierced crowd at **Piknic Électronik** (piknicelectronik.com), an outdoor rave held on Île Ste.-Hélène during the summer. At Jean-Drapeau Park, follow the slithering beats to *The Man*, a giant sculpture, created by Alexander Calder for the 1967 Expo, which hovers over the dance floor. The leafy island has other architectural ruins from the Expo. Between beats, stroll over to the **Montreal Biosphere** (biosphere.ec.gc.ca), the iconic geodesic dome that still evokes a utopian vision of technology.

OPPOSITE À Table Tout le Monde in Old Montreal.

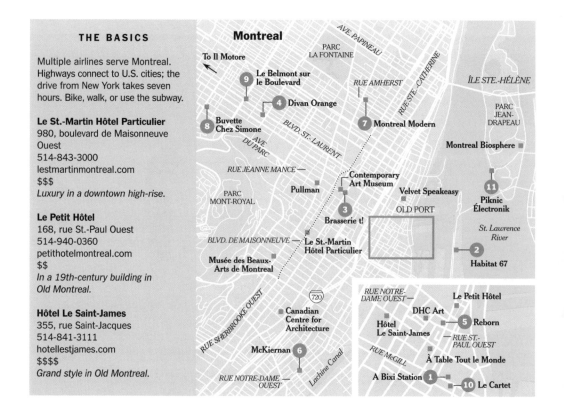

Mont Tremblant

One of the oldest ski resorts in North America, with miles of runs in the evergreen-topped Laurentian Mountains, Mont Tremblant, Quebec, seems to have it all. Combining the Canadian charm of a rustic logging town with the Old World flavor of the French Alps, Tremblant is consistently ranked by Ski Magazine readers as the East's No. 1 resort. Hotels, condos, and bed-and-breakfasts accommodate thousands of skiers, and there are enough restaurants, shops, pools, and spas to keep everyone busy after a day on the slopes. Mont Tremblant is a year-round resort, with golf courses, a casino, and a national park, but it is in winter, when 150 inches of snow keep the ski trails slippery and the rooftops white, that it really comes into its own. — BY LIONEL BEEHNER

FRIDAY

1 *Sleigh Bells Ring* 4 p.m.

For an action-packed lay of the land, hop on a sleigh ride with the resort's **Activity Center** (Place St. Bernard; 819-681-4848; tremblantactivities.com), which offers hourlong rides for 35 Canadian dollars (despite fluctuating currency rates, the prices usually aren't too different in U.S. dollars). Two beefy Percheron horses — steam wafting from their bodies — pull a rickety yet comfortable sleigh through Quebec's boreal forest, while the tour guide animatedly regales passengers with stories about the "trembling" mountain and may even sing some Québécois folk songs. The trip is like an Alpine safari; the trail is teeming with wildlife, like white-tail deer and red foxes. Bundle up — the mercury often dips below zero. Blankets are provided, and halfway through the ride everyone gulps down some hot cocoa.

2 *Alternative Shopping* 5 p.m.

Skip the resort's pricey boutiques and head to historic St.-Jovite — a village now rechristened Centre-Ville Mont-Tremblant — a 10-minute drive

OPPOSITE The base village at Mont Tremblant, widely considered to be the No. 1 ski resort in eastern North America.

RIGHT The shops of St.-Jovite, now called Centre-Ville Mont-Tremblant, are a 10-minute drive from the mountain.

from the mountain. Explore the shops on Rue St.-Jovite. **Plaisirs de Provence** (No. 814; 819-425-2000; plaisirsdeprovence.com) is a Québécois version of a Pottery Barn, with upscale dishware, cutlery, and chocolate. For handmade golf shoes and high-end ladies' footwear, drop by **Nycole St.-Louis Collections** (No. 822; 819-425-3583; nycolestlouis.com). Folk arts and country antiques are the specialty at **Le Coq Rouge** (No. 821; 819-425-3205).

3 *Poutine Time* 7 p.m.

Foodies will appreciate the Quebec-style fusion cooking at **sEb** (444 Rue St.-Georges; 819-429-6991; resto-seb.com; $$$). A high-end restaurant with a laid-back vibe, it gives comfort food a modern twist. Traditional dishes like rabbit stew or bison strip loin steak are jazzed up with local foie gras or the hefty regional favorite known as poutine, cheese curd with fries and gravy. Sébastien Houle, the young proprietor, cut his culinary teeth as a chef on the yacht of Paul Allen, a cofounder of Microsoft.

4 *Canadian Bandstand* 9 p.m.

Find Tremblant's young partyers at **P'tit Caribou** (125 Chemin de Kandahar; 819-681-4500; ptitcaribou.com), a dive bar in the base village with beer-soaked wooden floors and bar-top dancers. D.J.'s, popcorn, and low prices keep things lively,

and if the exuberance appears particularly youthful, recall that the legal drinking age in Quebec is 18.

SATURDAY

5 *French Breakfast* 7:30 a.m.

Kick off your day with something sweet. **Crêperie Catherine** (113 Chemin de Kandahar; 819-681-4888; creperiecatherine.ca; $$), carved out of a former chalet, is famous among local skiers for its old-fashioned crepes, and the hundreds of chef-themed dolls, teapots, cookie jars, and other tchotchkes that line its walls. Order the house specialty — a crepe with hot and velvety sucre à la crème. Arrive early. Seats here are in demand.

6 *Go North, Young Skier* 8:30 a.m.

Tremblant (819-681-2000; tremblant.ca) is a mountain folded in four parts, with a south, north and soleil (sunny) side and a segment called the Edge. Start the morning on the north side, when there is usually more sun and less wind. Long cruisers like Beauchemin let you find your balance before conquering the fast bumps on Saute-Moutons. After lunch, follow the sun over to the south side. Nansen offers marvelous views largely untainted by condos, while speed demons should hit the steeps of Kandahar. To ski off-piste, take the Telecabine Express gondola to the top and ski down to the Edge

lift, or trek over to the soleil side. Of Tremblant's 94 trails, 15 are glades. If the conditions get icy — this is the East Coast, after all — drop by the cozy Grand Manitou summit restaurant. Or just high-tail it back to your condo's hot tub.

7 *Aprés-Ski Sweets* 3:30 p.m.

Polish off a long day of skiing with a beavertail. Basically it consists of a whole wheat pastry deep-fried, smothered with your choice of maple syrup or Nutella and shaped like, yup, a beaver's tail. Drop by the takeout window at **Queues de Castor** (116 Chemin de Kandahar; 819-681-4678).

8 *Nordic Thaw* 5 p.m.

Landed a few face plants? Pamper those sore muscles at **Le Scandinave** (4280 Montée Ryan; 819-425-5524; scandinave.com), a Nordic-themed spa in a barnlike fortress on the outskirts of town. The spa's rustic-chic motif and thermal waterfalls will

ABOVE Mont Tremblant National Park, vast and just outside town, is laced with waterways and comes alive in summer with canoeing, hiking, and fishing.

OPPOSITE ABOVE AND BELOW Pampering is available indoors and out at Le Scandinave, a Nordic-themed spa. Warm up in a hot bath before plunging into the icy Diable River, or stick to the massages and thermal waterfalls inside.

lull bathers into a state of relaxation. Warm up in a Finnish sauna or Norwegian steam bath before taking a cold plunge in the Diable River out back. Sadly, the 17,000-square-foot spa doesn't offer maple syrup scrubs like some of its competitors. But a Swedish massage will rejuvenate even the sorest of muscles. Take it from two of the owners, who are retired NHL hockey players.

9 *Slopeside Fondue* 7:30 p.m.

"Have you tried the fondue at La Savoie?" You'll hear that question a lot in Mont Tremblant. In the middle of the base village, **La Savoie** (115 Chemin de Kandahar; 819-681-4573; restaurantlasavoie. com; $$$) has a homey décor befitting a chateau in the Savoy region in the French Alps. The same

goes for the fondue. Tabletop pierrades and raclettes let patrons cook up their own shrimp, chicken, fish, or filet mignon in communal fashion, before dunking the morsels into melted cheeses, red wine, or garlic sauces. Chances are you won't have room for the chocolate fondue.

10 *Hockey-Free Zone* 9:30 p.m.

Most bars in town, it seems, are just repositories of wall-mounted moose heads and bad cover bands. A welcome exception is **La Diable** (117 Chemin de

Kandahar; 819-681-4546), a low-key microbrasserie that serves up an eclectic array of devil-themed brews like the Extreme Onction—a Belgian Trappist-style ale with 8.5 percent alcohol. La Diable might also be the only mountainside bar without hockey playing on the flat screen.

Nordic Adventure Dog Sledding (Place St. Bernard; 819-681-4848; tremblantactivities.com). After a 40-minute bus ride, you arrive at what looks like the setting of a Jack London novel—a secluded camp in the woods surrounded by nothing but Siberian huskies. Above the din of barking dogs, the gregarious guide explains how to steer and how to stop and go ("Hop-hop!" or "Mush!"). Eight harness-linked dogs sprint at breakneck speed. The two-hour ride (about 150 Canadian dollars) winds its way through some challenging terrain, interrupted only by a cabin break for hot chocolate and a prep course in fire-starting.

SUNDAY

11 *Call of the Wild* 8:15 a.m.

Ever wanted to commandeer a caravan of canines through the Canadian wilderness? Pay a visit to

ABOVE AND OPPOSITE Skiing is the preferred way to play outside, but there are others. One option is dogsledding in Mont Tremblant's reliable fresh snow, with you in the driver's seat. Count on the guide to teach you when to say "Mush!"

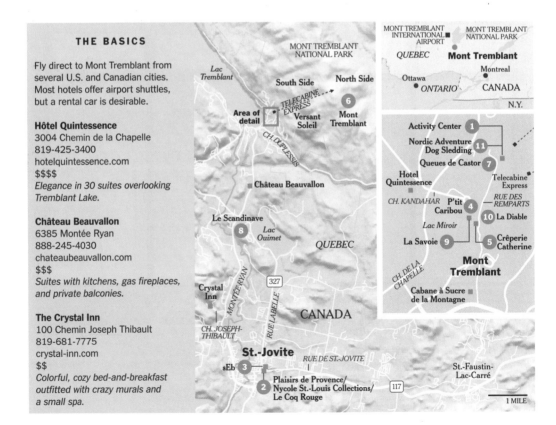

THE BASICS

Fly direct to Mont Tremblant from several U.S. and Canadian cities. Most hotels offer airport shuttles, but a rental car is desirable.

Hôtel Quintessence
3004 Chemin de la Chapelle
819-425-3400
hotelquintessence.com
$$$$
Elegance in 30 suites overlooking Tremblant Lake.

Château Beauvallon
6385 Montée Ryan
888-245-4030
chateaubeauvallon.com
$$$
Suites with kitchens, gas fireplaces, and private balconies.

The Crystal Inn
100 Chemin Joseph Thibault
819-681-7775
crystal-inn.com
$$
Colorful, cozy bed-and-breakfast outfitted with crazy murals and a small spa.

Quebec City

Quebec can give provincialism a good name. Orphaned by mother France, dominated by Britain (after what Québécois still call the Conquest) and then for years by majority-Anglophone Canada, the people of Quebec have followed Voltaire's advice to tend to their own garden. This is especially true of Quebec City, the provincial capital. Proudly dated, lovingly maintained, Quebec City has charm to spare, particularly within the city walls of the Old Town and in the Lower Town tucked between those walls and the St. Lawrence River. The city's French heart is always on its sleeve, and a stroll over the cobblestones leads to patisseries, sidewalk cafes, and a profusion of art galleries. Yet a vast, cold wilderness is the next stop due north, putting game on restaurant menus and a kind of backwoods vigor in the city's spirit. To a Yankee it all seems European. But there is no place like this in Europe; there is nothing else like it in North America, either. And that's reason enough to celebrate.

— BY SCOTT L. MALCOMSON

FRIDAY

1 *Champagne and Cigars* 6 p.m.

It's too late in the day to head out for kayaking on the St. Lawrence River, so go instead to the first-floor **St. Laurent Bar & Lounge** at the **Fairmont Le Château Frontenac** (1, rue des Carrières; 418-692-3861; fairmont.com/frontenac) for Champagne. You're atop the city's cliffs, and this semicircular room has wonderful views of the St. Lawrence. A drink in the château, as it is called (it's that enormous castle-like building, built as a grand hotel for the Canadian Pacific Railway) is always pricey, but luxury can be like that. Even the bar food is classy, running to snacks like assiette of smoked fish. If all this old-money atmosphere makes you crave a Cuban cigar, buy a supply at **Société Cigare** (575, Grande Allée; 418-647-2000), just outside the Old Town walls. It is also a bar (dark wood, low lights, single malts), so it's open most of the time.

2 *Lower Town Update* 8 p.m.

Fast-forward a few decades by finding your way down to St. Roch in the Lower Town, hard up against the cliff. Once a grim commercial district, it has evolved into a hotspot of high-tech businesses,

artists' studios, galleries, shops, and cafés. One of the pioneering restaurants in the transformation was the sleek **Versa** (432, rue du Parvis; 418-523-9995; versarestaurant.com; $$$), which touts its mojitos and boasts that it is the city's only oyster bar. The menu mixes bistro food and more formal entrees like poached swordfish or veal sweetbreads and roasted cheek.

3 *Dancing Feet* 10 p.m.

For a taste of St. Roch nightlife, drop in at **Le Boudoir** (441, rue de l'Église; 418-524-2777; boudoirlounge.com), a bar packed with young professionals. D.J.'s keep things hopping on the weekends, and the sound system boasts 60 speakers. There's dancing on the lower level.

SATURDAY

4 *On the Plains* 10 a.m.

Take a jog or a leisurely walk on the **Plains of Abraham**, an extensive, undulating rectangle on the heights above the St. Lawrence just west of the Frontenac. This is where British invaders led by James Wolfe defeated Louis-Joseph de Montcalm in 1759, the battle that set in motion the decline of French power in North America. Today it is a playground, an urban park (ccbn-nbc.gc.ca) where children race around

OPPOSITE The guards at Quebec's Citadel may look English, but their regiment's official language is French.

BELOW For tourists, walking is the way to get around.

the open spaces, actors stroll by in 18th-century garb, skiers glide in winter, and Paul McCartney gave a free concert in 2008 to mark Quebec City's 400th birthday. For a concrete example of Quebec's mixed historical legacy, stop off at the **Citadel** (1, Côte de la Citadelle; 418-694-2815; lacitadelle.qc.ca), where an officially French-speaking regiment performs an English-style changing of the guard, complete with black bearskin hats, every summer morning at 10.

5 *Market Bounty* Noon

The farmers' market (**Marché du Vieux-Port**; 160, Quai Saint-André, near the old train station; 418-692-2517; marchevieuxport.com) is open year-round. In summer there's an abundance of fresh vegetables and fruits. Even in winter, you can find local cheeses, meat pies, fish, sausage, baked goods, and foie gras. Look for spruce beer, which George Washington is reported to have served to his troops for medicinal reasons. One taste and you'll see why: it is the poor colonist's retsina.

6 *Provincial Special* 2 p.m.

At least once this weekend you have to eat poutine, the concoction of French fries, cheese curd, and gravy that is close to the French Canadian soul, if not particularly friendly to its heart. Find it at **Buffet de l'Antiquaire** (95, rue St.-Paul; 418-692-2661; $), a Lower Town institution with sidewalk tables in summer. It is a very good, very local diner that serves all kinds of Canadian comfort food and is always worth a visit at breakfast, too.

7 *That Perfect Find* 3 p.m.

Walk out into the rue St.-Paul, a street lined with easygoing antiques shops and art galleries, to poke through Victoriana, country furniture, Art Deco relics, and assorted gewgaws. If you still can't find the right present to take home, take the first

ABOVE The Lower Town along the St. Lawrence River.

LEFT J.A. Moisan, a gourmet grocery store.

OPPOSITE The Château Frontenac is now a Fairmont Hotel.

left up into the Old Town and head for **Artisans du Bas-Canada** (30, côte de la Fabrique; 418-692-2109; artisanscanada.com), which has jewelry made from Canadian diamonds and amber as well as an abundance of Québécois tchotchkes.

8 *Take to the Ramparts* 6 p.m.

Stroll along the ramparts of the Old Town for a stirring view of the St. Lawrence. Quebec City was strategic because of its commanding position on the river just at the point where it begins to widen and grow into the Gulf of St. Lawrence on its way to the Atlantic. Then proceed downhill for a drink at the friendly and cozy **Belley Tavern** (249, rue St.-Paul; 418-692-1694). Or try **Môss** (225, rue St.-Paul; 418-692-0233), a "bistro belge" that has a wide selection of Belgian beers, including several on tap, and many ways of preparing mussels.

9 *Haute Cuisine* 8 p.m.

Most Québécois speak English, but French, even bad French, goes over well. So use yours to ask for directions to the luxury hotel called **Auberge Saint-Antoine** (8, rue St.-Antoine). Its restaurant, **Panache** (418-692-2211; restaurantpanache.com; $$$$), is a point of reference for Quebec City's haute cuisine. Start off with Champagne cocktails, then on to an amuse-bouche and the tasting menu, which moves at a leisurely pace from an appetizer, perhaps foie gras, through seafood and meats that often include venison or other Canadian game, and finally to dessert, all with suitable wines. It is easy to drag this out — in a space that is like a rustic loft with upholstered chairs — for three hours or more. After dinner, make your way through the narrow streets to admire the restored buildings of the Place-Royal at your leisure.

SUNDAY

10 *Riverside* 11 a.m.

You've gazed at the St. Lawrence from the heights; now it's time to get close. Join the locals catching the breeze on the **Promenade Samuel de Champlain**, a riverfront strip park that opened in 2008, in time for the city's 400th anniversary celebration. The 1.5-mile-long promenade, on land between the boulevard Champlain and the river—for many years a degraded industrial

area—was such a hit that the city soon set to work extending it to a length that will eventually reach for six more miles.

11 *One Last Chance* Noon

If you're still in the market for something to take home, check out **J.A. Moisan** (699, rue Saint-Jean; 418-522-0685; jamoisan.com), which claims to be the oldest gourmet grocery store in North America. Should the cheeses, chocolates, pasta, and other fare fail to charm, you'll find a selection of other high-end shops on rue Saint-Jean.

ABOVE AND OPPOSITE Quebec City's charming Old Town.

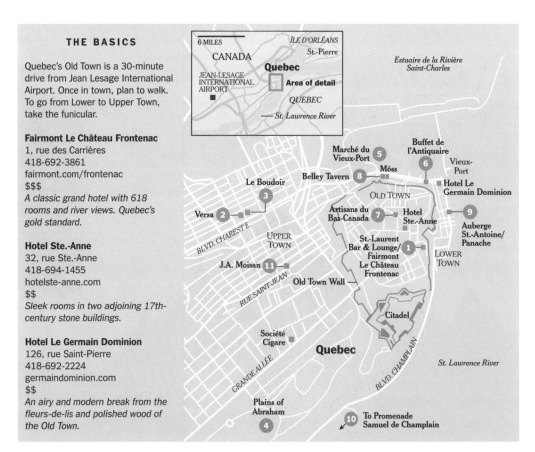

THE BASICS

Quebec's Old Town is a 30-minute drive from Jean Lesage International Airport. Once in town, plan to walk. To go from Lower to Upper Town, take the funicular.

Fairmont Le Château Frontenac
1, rue des Carrières
418-692-3861
fairmont.com/frontenac
$$$
A classic grand hotel with 618 rooms and river views. Quebec's gold standard.

Hotel Ste.-Anne
32, rue Ste.-Anne
418-694-1455
hotelste-anne.com
$$
Sleek rooms in two adjoining 17th-century stone buildings.

Hotel Le Germain Dominion
126, rue Saint-Pierre
418-692-2224
germaindominion.com
$$
An airy and modern break from the fleurs-de-lis and polished wood of the Old Town.

The Bay of Fundy

At Fundy National Park in New Brunswick, the salty ocean air is laced with the scent of pine. The park's smooth lakes and quiet forests alone would be enough to make it one of Canada's favorites. But the real wonder here is a strange natural phenomenon: the sweeping tides of the Bay of Fundy. Residents around the bay say its tides are the highest in the world, and only a bay in far northern Quebec challenges the claim; the Canadian government diplomatically calls it a tie. Highest or not, the Fundy tides are extreme and dramatic, rising at their largest surge by 33 feet and leaving, when they recede, vast tidal flats ready for exploring. Tourists who drive north through New Brunswick on their way to Fundy will be struck by the forests stretching to the horizon and by the comfortable mix of French and English influences that has cashiers and waitresses calling out "Hello bonjour!"
— BY KAREN HOUPPERT

FRIDAY

1 *Park Central* 3 p.m.

The main attraction is **Fundy National Park** (506-887-6000; pc.gc.ca/eng/pn-np/nb/fundy/index.aspx), which covers about 50,000 acres and is laced with trails and sprinkled with campsites that make it a paradise for backpackers. Away from the hub of activity around the park headquarters (and not counting the surprising presence of a nine-hole golf course), there are few tourist services. Get your bearings at the **Visitor Reception Centre**, close to the southeastern park entrance near the gateway town of Alma. Pick up maps, find out about the interpretive programs for the weekend, and most important, check the tide tables.

2 *Fundy Fare* 6 p.m.

Drive into Alma for dinner (there's no dining in the park itself). You'll find lobster with a view at the **Tides Restaurant**, located in the **Parkland Village Inn** (8601 Main Street, Alma; 506-887-2313;

OPPOSITE AND RIGHT Fundy National Park's 68 miles of well-tended trails wind into forests and meadows, past waterfalls and beaver dams. Although spectacular tides, rising 33 feet, are the area's major attraction, the park is also prized for its inland natural beauty.

parklandvillageinn.com; $$), where the dining room overlooks the bay. The choices run to the traditional and hearty, including steaks and various kinds of Atlantic seafood, good for packing it in at the start of an active weekend. Tables at the Tides can fill up fast, so take care to reserve in advance.

3 *Brushwork* 7 p.m.

Fundy's vast, muddy stretches of beach mean that even high tide makes for poor swimming. The water remains shallow for a quarter mile out to sea. The park does its best to compensate, offering visitors a swim in its heated salt-water pool overlooking the bay. But if the Bay of Fundy is not great for swimming, it is a sensuous delight. As evening approaches, stroll along the coastal paths to take it in. At dusk, as the fog rolls in, the hills and cliffs beyond the shore shimmer with the deep green of thousands of pines. The silky-smooth red clay of the tidal flat provides a rich saturation of complementary color. It's like stepping into a Van Gogh.

SATURDAY

4 *Sticky Fingers* 9 a.m.

You could go for the fresh home-baked bread or doughnuts, or come back at lunch for sandwiches and chili, but the star of the show at **Kelly's Bake Shop**

(8587 Main Street, Alma; 506-887-2460) is the sticky bun. Locally renowned and alluring for tourists, the buns keep customers lined up at Kelly's, which sells as many as 3,000 of them on a busy day. They're sweet, flavorful, and enormous. Don't expect to eat more than one.

5 *Reset the Clock* 9:30 a.m.

Venture to one of Alma's two small general stores to pick up provisions for later. Then consult your new clock, the lunar version that announces itself in the Fundy tides. It's important to be at the beach when the mud flats are exposed — that's the experience that draws people here. So plan your day accordingly — not by the numbers on your watch or cellphone, but by the water's flow.

6 *Out to Sea* Low Tide

At low tide the vast intertidal zone is other-worldly: endless red muddy flats, shallow pools and sporadic, massive barnacle-covered boulders that appear to have been randomly dropped into the muddy flatness from an alien spaceship. Beachcombers can walk along the exposed ocean floor, hunting for shells and bits of sea-smoothed glass, for more than half a mile before they reach the water's edge. The impulse to scoop up the clay underfoot and squeeze it through your fingers is hard to suppress. While grown-up travelers seem to enjoy the delightful respite the wet clay of the bare ocean floor provides to tired feet after a hard day of hiking, kids have been known to do full body rolls in the squishy muck. The spot where you're standing will probably be under water again before long, but there's no need to fear. The tide's return is gradual, progressive, and orderly — very Canadian — and nicely nudges you back shoreward with small, gentle, very cold waves.

7 *Into the Woods* High Tide

When the water claims the beach, go hiking. The park's 68 miles of well-tended trails wind deep into

forests and flower-strewn meadows, past waterfalls and beaver dams, and even to a covered bridge. By the standards of many busier parks, it is blissfully quiet. Even in August, the prime season, it is possible for hikers to trek the 2.8-mile **Mathews Head** trail along the park's rocky southern shore and not pass a single person. The path offers teasing ocean views from atop cliffs that drop to the sea. And amid the solitude, there is a silence so pervasive that even children grow pensive at the wonder of these head-lands, which feel like the end of the earth.

8 *Shell and Claw* 7 p.m.

Do as the locals do and find a table at the **Harbour View Market & Restaurant** (8598 Main Street, Alma; 506-887-2450; $). You can get your daily ration of shell-fish — in the seafood chowder or a lobster roll — and perhaps pick up some local gossip at the same time.

9 *Nature Theater* 8 p.m.

Don't look for rangers at Fundy National Park — here they are interpreters. The staff is serious about the job of making Fundy accessible, and in summer there is a program almost every night at the **Outdoor Theatre**. You may learn about the wildlife, from moose and bears to flying squirrels. You may hear about the rivers that wash kayakers upstream when the tide comes in, the whales and migratory

birds that thrive offshore, or the area's history—this is Acadia, where French and English cultures clashed and mingled. Expect a multimedia experience, with video, music, comedy, or even drama.

SUNDAY

10 *Water Power* 10 a.m.

For an appropriate last stop, drive about 25 miles north of Alma to Hopewell Cape, where the bay shore is littered with eroded sea stacks known as the **Flowerpot Rocks**. See them from a clifftop trail, and if it's low tide inspect them close up, at the **Hopewell Rocks Ocean Tidal Exploration Site** (Highway 114; 877-734-3429; thehopewellrocks.ca). Resembling pillars or top-heavy mushrooms, some with trees growing on their tops, the rocks are part of a rugged shoreline of caves, tunnels, and misshapen crags, all

of it a testament to the relentless force of the water constantly tugged back and forth against the shore by the Fundy tides.

OPPOSITE ABOVE The world's highest tides (officially tied with those in a more remote Quebec bay) flow out to leave vast flats for exploring.

OPPOSITE BELOW Mathews Head, a high rocky headland on the Fundy coast.

ABOVE A sunrise over Owl's Head, seen from Alma Beach in Fundy National Park.

THE BASICS

Fundy National Park is a drive of three hours from the Maine-New Brunswick border and an hour and a half from the airport in Moncton, New Brunswick. A car is essential.

Fundy Highlands Inn and Chalets
8714 Route 114
506-887-2930
fundyhighlandchalets.com
$$
Motel rooms and colorful cabins within Fundy National Park.

Falcon Ridge Inn
24 Falcon Ridge Drive, Alma
506-887-1110
falconridgeinn.nb.ca
$$
A B&B built in 2000.

Cliffside Suites and Cottage
22 Bayview Drive, Alma
506-887-1022
cliffsidesuites.com
$$
Minutes from the park.

Halifax

Halifax, Nova Scotia, is a harbor city steeped in maritime history. Founded in 1749 as a British naval and military base, it originally served as a strategic counter to French bases elsewhere in Atlantic Canada—and many years later as an assembly point for shipping convoys during World Wars I and II. Today, Halifax is better known for its lobster, which you can fill up on from morning (lobster eggs Benedict, anyone?) till night and still have enough cash left for a sail around the harbor on a tall ship. A vibrant student population—the city's several universities have thousands of students—gives Halifax a youthful, bohemian feel, too. As a result, it's often compared to that other hilly town on the ocean, San Francisco, but you'll find that Halifax's blend of fair-trade coffee bars, wharfside lobster shacks, and public gardens has a character all its own.

— BY TATIANA BONCOMPAGNI

FRIDAY

1 *A Pint and a Pirate Joke* 5 p.m.

Start the weekend right at the **Alexander Keith's Nova Scotia Brewery** (1496 Lower Water Street; 902-455-1474; keiths.ca). Take the 55-minute tour led by local actors in 19th-century garb, and you'll get not only a primer on the history of Halifax's oldest working brewery—it dates back to the 1820s—but a pint of its finest as well. Find a comfy bench in the brewery's Stag's Head Tavern, where barkeepers have been known to regale the crowd with old pirate jokes and barmaids have burst into song.

2 *Bard of Nova Scotia* 7 p.m.

Shakespeare is so much better in the grass, methinks. Grab a blanket and some cushions and head to **Point Pleasant Park** (Queen Victoria leased it to Halifax around the mid-19th century for one shilling a year, which the city still pays), where the **Shakespeare by the Sea Theater Society** (902-422-0295; shakespearebythesea.ca) stages the Bard's plays. The

OPPOSITE The *Bluenose II*, a replica of the schooner on the back of the Canadian dime, docked on the waterfront. Halifax's natural harbor is one of the world's largest.

RIGHT Firing the noon-day gun at Halifax Citadel.

park overlooks the entrance to Halifax Harbor, so enjoy the sublime views, then arrive for the performance 10 minutes before show time and stake your claim in the grass. A $15 donation is encouraged.

3 *Bring Your Own Shoes* 10 p.m.

For a late meal, a sophisticated spot is the **Economy Shoe Shop** (1663 Argyle Street; 902-423-7463; economyshoeshop.ca; $-$$), a cafe and bar that takes its name from a salvaged neon sign hanging from the side of its building. It is divided into four sections —Shoe, Backstage, Diamond, and Oasis—based on décor. Ask to be seated in Oasis, a comparatively quiet nook in the back of the building. Honor Haligonian tradition by ordering seafood chowder or fish cakes.

SATURDAY

4 *Breakfast on the Commons* 9:30 a.m.

In the 18th century, town authorities set aside more than 200 acres for community cattle grazing and military use. The part that remains, called the Commons, is a municipal complex of sports fields and playgrounds—a great place for a morning jog. But for those who would rather slip into the day more gently, there's **jane's on the common** (2394 Robie Street; 902-431-5683; janesonthecommon.com; $$), which serves a killer brunch from 9:30 a.m. to 2:30 p.m. on weekends. The ricotta pancakes with fresh bananas and Nova Scotia maple syrup are light and

fluffy, the eggs come with sausage or fish, and there's tofu for the vegans.

5 *Antiquing on Agricola* 10:30 a.m.

If you're in the market for well-priced antiques or reproductions, make sure you hit Agricola Street, where a handful of the city's best dealers have set up shop. At **McLellan Antiques & Restoration** (2738 Agricola Street; 902-455-4545; mclellanantiques.com) you'll find furniture including bureaus and cupboards, early pine pieces, and 1920s mahogany. **Finer Things Antiques** (2797 Agricola Street; 902-456-1412; finerthingsantiques.com) is the place to go for nautical antiques like old ship's wheels and compasses.

6 *Sail On* 1 p.m.

No trip to Halifax is complete without a tour around the harbor — considered the second-largest natural harbor anywhere, after Sydney's — in one of the tall ships that dock along the wharf. Sign up for a two-hour sail aboard the ***Bluenose II*** (1675 Lower Water Street, 902-634-1963; halifaxkiosk.com/Bluenose-II.php), a replica of the schooner that earned its spot on the Canadian dime by collecting numerous racing trophies in the 1920s and '30s. It has a 4,150-square-foot mainsail and a top speed of 16 knots. If the *Bluenose II* isn't in town — its home port is Lunenburg, about 60 miles away, and it travels along the Maritime and New England coasts — sail the harbor aboard the ***Silva*** (tallshipsilva.com) or the ***Mar II*** (mtcw.ca/TourSailing.php). Dress warmly; it can get cold on deck.

7 *Remembrance* 5 p.m.

Halifax's role as a busy port city, sometimes complicated by the North Atlantic's infamous fog, has cursed it with a legacy of shipwrecks and catastrophe. The **Maritime Museum of the Atlantic** (1675 Lower Water Street; 902-424-7490; museum.gov.ns.ca/mma/) has moving displays of artifacts from them. One commemorates the disaster most horrific for Halifax. It happened in 1917, when a French ship loaded with explosives collided in the harbor with a Belgian relief ship, resulting in a blast that killed nearly 2,000 people, injured thousands more, and obliterated the north end of the city. The museum also displays an incredibly well-preserved deck chair from the *Titanic*, which sank off the Grand Banks in 1912. Of the 328 bodies recovered from the *Titanic*, 150 are buried in Halifax.

8 *Menu Study* 8 p.m.

Make your way to the neighborhood of Dalhousie University's downtown Sexton campus for dinner at **Chives Canadian Bistro**, (1537 Barrington Street; 902-420-9626; chives.ca/about; $$$). Its imaginative

dishes are made with local and seasonal ingredients, so selections change. Scan the menu for dishes like pan-seared Nova Scotia sea bass or classic coq au vin on egg yolk fettucine.

SUNDAY

9 *The Citadel* 11 a.m.

The best views in the city can be had from the **Halifax Citadel** (5425 Sackville Street; 902-426-5080; pc.gc.ca/lhn-nhs/ns/halifax/index.aspx), a star-shaped fort built on its highest hill. The British built four forts atop the summit, the last of which was completed in 1856, when the United States posed

ABOVE Homage to the original brewmaster at Alexander Keith's Nova Scotia Brewery.

the greatest threat to the harbor and city. Be sure to get there in time for the "noon-day gun" firing of the cannon. Afterward watch pipers and drummers perform in the enormous gravel courtyard.

10 *Last Call for Lobster* 1 p.m.

It wouldn't be right to leave without a taste of sweet Nova Scotia lobster. Snag an umbrella-shaded outdoor table at **Salty's** (1869 Upper Water Street; 902-423-6818; saltys.ca; $$-$$$). Go for a steamed one-and-a-half-pounder and a side of hot sweet-potato fries, and you won't be hungry on the plane going home.

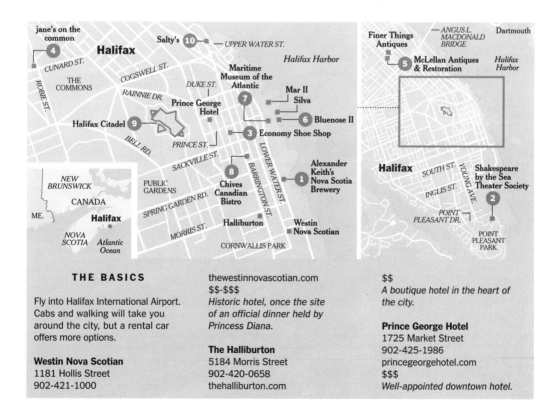

THE BASICS

Fly into Halifax International Airport. Cabs and walking will take you around the city, but a rental car offers more options.

Westin Nova Scotian
1181 Hollis Street
902-421-1000

thewestinnovascotian.com
$$-$$$
Historic hotel, once the site of an official dinner held by Princess Diana.

The Halliburton
5184 Morris Street
902-420-0658
thehalliburton.com

$$
A boutique hotel in the heart of the city.

Prince George Hotel
1725 Market Street
902-425-1986
princegeorgehotel.com
$$$
Well-appointed downtown hotel.

St. John's

Founded in the late 16th century on North America's easternmost edge, St. John's was already a settlement when New York was a mere gleam in the eye of European colonizers. Cod was king then and for centuries afterward, and although now it's the offshore oil industry that brings in cash and confidence, the city has hung onto its unique, quirky character. Brightly colored row houses cascade down toward the harbor, not far from where icebergs, whales, and puffins pass by in summer. George Street is the North Atlantic version of Bourbon Street. And as the capital of the Canadian province of Newfoundland and Labrador, St. John's shares in the region's typical friendliness but keeps its own decidedly Irish twist—many locals speak with the thickest brogues west of Galway. — BY JEFF SCHLEGEL

FRIDAY

1 *It Happened Out There* 3:30 p.m.

An ideal first stop is Signal Hill, a rocky sentinel that overlooks the entrance to the harbor. Before reaching the top, though, visit the **Johnson Geo Centre** (175 Signal Hill Road; 709-737-7880; geocentre.ca), where one exhibit tells the tale of the sinking of the *Titanic* 350 miles off this coast. The ship's radio distress signals were picked up by Newfoundland stations, and St. John's has been a frequent departure point for explorers' trips to the wreck. Shake your head in disbelief as you read about the decision not to equip the ship with enough lifeboats because it would "clutter up the deck." Atop Signal Hill looms **Cabot Tower** (pc.gc.ca/lhn-nhs/nl/signalhill), a castle-like structure next to where Marconi received the first trans-Atlantic wireless message in 1901. At the lookout point, take in a sweeping view.

2 *Cod Tongues, Anyone?* 6 p.m.

Velma's Place (264 Water Street; 709-576-2264; $) specializes in healthy helpings of traditional cuisine. An appetizer of cod tongues with scrunchions, or fat pork, and a meal of baked cod au gratin or fish and

OPPOSITE St. John's, Newfoundland and Labrador. European ships have used its harbor since the early 1500s.

RIGHT Climb to the top of Signal Hill for sweeping views.

chips made with cod is as Newfoundland as it gets. Home-cooked food is the rule, and the hot turkey sandwich is made with real roast turkey with dark meat, not bland deli meat.

3 *Off Off Off Broadway* 8 p.m.

Take in a play at the newly refurbished **Resource Center for the Arts** in the former Longshoremen's Protective Union Hall (3 Victoria Street; 709-753-4531; rca.nf.ca). The center hosts theater and dance. It is also a venue for art shows ranging from experimental to traditional, particularly promoting emerging artists in Newfoundland and Labrador.

4 *Have a Cow, Man* 10 p.m.

For a post-show treat, visit **Moo-Moo's Ice Cream** (88 Kings Road; 709-753-3046), a boxy building painted a mottled black and white in dairy-cow fashion. The store makes more than 300 flavors of ice cream in its basement factory, and serves them upstairs. Two of the favorites are turtle cheesecake—a mix of cheesecake, Oreo crumbs, and English toffee—and the chocolate-heavy tornado, which is made with Mirage candy bars, a Canadian favorite.

SATURDAY

5 *Coffee and Crumpets* 9 a.m.

Fuel up on an espresso drink or the house brew at **Coffee Matters** (1 Military Road; 709-753-6980;

coffeematters.ca; $) in a neat frame building down-
town. Hot drinks are the stars here. Besides the usual
lattes, macchiato, and house brews, there's a selection
of hot chocolates, including banana silk and Aztec. This
is a coffee house, but you can settle in for a sit-down
breakfast. Besides the usual waffles and eggs, there's
the crumpet sandwich. That's egg, sausage, and
cheese on — that's right, a crumpet.

6 *Trailing the Puffin* 11 a.m.

After breakfast, drive about half an hour south
to **Bay Bulls** (Highway 2 south to Highway 3, which
merges into Highway 10 south). **Gatherall's Puffin &
Whale Watch** (Northside Road; 709-334-2887;
gatheralls.com) is one of the eco-tour operators
in town that ferry passengers to the Witless Bay
Ecological Reserve, a group of offshore islands that
in summer are host to 2.5 million mating seabirds,
including about 500,000 puffins. Whales also appear
in the bay during their summer migration and, if the
currents are right, you might see an iceberg or two
floating down from Greenland.

7 *Provincial Culture* 3 p.m.

It's hard to miss the **Rooms** (9 Bonaventure
Avenue; 709-757-8000; therooms.ca), a huge
museum and art gallery that towers above the
city from a hilltop perch. Designed to resemble
traditional Newfoundland fishing rooms where

families processed their catch, the Rooms combines
the Provincial Museum, the Provincial Art Gallery,
and the Provincial Archives under one roof. The
spotlight is on artists from Newfoundland and
Labrador and elsewhere in Canada. Unofficially,
among its best displays is the view of the harbor's
meeting with the Atlantic at Signal Hill.

8 *Pews and Stouts* 5 p.m.

The **Ship Pub** (Solomon's Lane at 265 Duckworth
Street; 709-753-3870) is a classic watering hole with
a laid-back vibe. There are several tables scattered
about and a lot of old wood, including church pews
set along the walls. It's easy to belly up to the time-
worn bar and chat up the barkeepers or the mix of
locals ranging from artists to lawyers. "It's just not a
pub," one customer said. "It's a living room."

9 *Nouvelle Caribou* 7 p.m.

After a drink or two, it's time for dinner. **Bacalao**
— the name means salted codfish — gives
Newfoundland and Labrador food an upscale nouvelle
Canadian twist (65 Lemarchant Road; 709-579-6565;
bacalaocuisine.ca; $$$). There's a salt cod dish of the
day, and the caribou medallions may arrive with a
sauce of Canadian fruit wine and partridgeberries,

ABOVE Cape Spear's 1955 lighthouse.

a native fruit and local favorite. Vegetarians are not forgotten; look for pasta with locally grown vegetables in season.

10 *Irish Energy* 9 p.m.

Downtown, George Street is party central, a stretch of pedestrian-only mayhem jammed with loud bars, dance spots, and clubs for Irish music, starting around 10:30 p.m. On a Saturday night at **Bridie Molloy's Pub & Eatery** (5 George Street; 709-576-5990), an acoustic trio played to the accompaniment of an Irish step dancer. Over at **O'Reilly's Irish Newfoundland Pub** (15 George Street; 709-722-3735; oreillyspub.com), a band with electric guitars played a more raucous set of Irish-tinged music.

SUNDAY

11 *Is That Europe Yonder?* 10 a.m.

You can't get much farther east in North America than **Cape Spear National Historic Site** (709-772-5367; pc.gc.ca/lhn-nhs/nl/spear/index.aspx). Follow Water Street southwest, turn left on Leslie Street, and find the sign for Cape Spear Drive. The drive passes through rugged terrain until it meets the ocean. There are two lighthouses—the original from 1836 and one built in 1955. You can pick up the **East Coast Trail** (eastcoasttrail.com) at the parking lot and hike south along the high sea cliffs. Imagine the sails of the ships that began arriving here soon after John Cabot found the rich nearby fishing grounds in 1497.

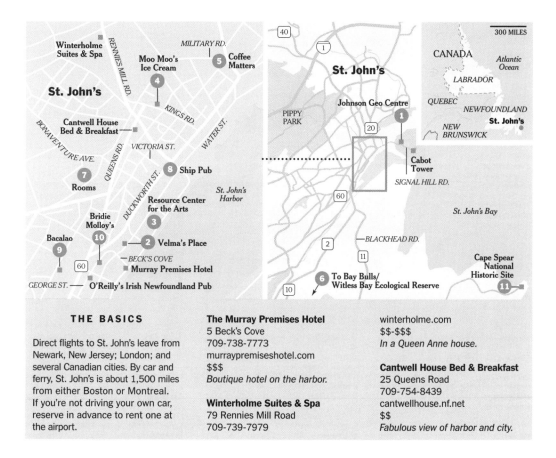

THE BASICS

Direct flights to St. John's leave from Newark, New Jersey; London; and several Canadian cities. By car and ferry, St. John's is about 1,500 miles from either Boston or Montreal. If you're not driving your own car, reserve in advance to rent one at the airport.

The Murray Premises Hotel
5 Beck's Cove
709-738-7773
murraypremiseshotel.com
$$$
Boutique hotel on the harbor.

Winterholme Suites & Spa
79 Rennies Mill Road
709-739-7979

winterholme.com
$$-$$$
In a Queen Anne house.

Cantwell House Bed & Breakfast
25 Queens Road
709-754-8439
cantwellhouse.nf.net
$$
Fabulous view of harbor and city.

Indexes

Additional photo credits: Steve Dunwell/ The Image Bank/Getty Images, 6; Gallo Images/Getty Images, 4; Stan Grossfeld/The Boston Globe, 100; City of St. John's, 162.

Acknowledgments

We would like to thank everyone at *The New York Times* and at TASCHEN who contributed to the creation of this book.

For the book project itself, special recognition must go to Nina Wiener and Eric Schwartau at TASCHEN, the dedicated editor and assistant behind the scenes; to Natasha Perkel, the *Times* artist whose clear and elegantly crafted maps make the itineraries comprehensible; to Phyllis Collazo of the *Times* staff, whose photo editing gave the book its arresting images; and to Olimpia Zagnoli, whose illustrations and illustrated maps enliven every article and each regional introduction.

Guiding the deft and artful transformation of newspaper material to book form at TASCHEN were Marco Zivny, the book's designer; Josh Baker, the art director; and Jennifer Patrick, production manager. Also at TASCHEN, David Martinez, Jessica Sappenfeld, Anna-Tina Kessler, Kirstin Plate and Janet Kim provided production assistance, and at the *Times*, Heidi Giovine helped at critical moments. Craig B. Gaines copy-edited the manuscript.

But the indebtedness goes much further back. This book grew out of the work of all of the editors, writers, photographers, and *Times* staff people whose contributions and support for the weekly "36 Hours" column built a rich archive over many years.

For this legacy, credit must go first to Stuart Emmrich, who created the column in 2002 and then refined the concept and guided its development over eight years, first as the *Times* Escapes editor and then as Travel editor. Without his vision, there would be no "36 Hours."

Great thanks must go to all of the writers and photographers whose work appears in the book, both *Times* staffers and freelancers.

And a legion of *Times* editors behind the scenes made it all happen, and still do.

Danielle Mattoon, who took over as Travel editor in 2010, has brought her steady hand to "36 Hours," and found time to be supportive of this book as well.

Suzanne MacNeille, now the column's direct editor, and her predecessors Jeff Z. Klein and Denny Lee have all superbly filled the role of finding and working with writers, choosing and assigning destinations, and assuring that the weekly product would entertain and inform readers while upholding *Times* journalistic standards. The former Escapes editors Amy Virshup and Mervyn Rothstein saw the column through many of its early years, assuring its consistent quality.

The talented *Times* photo editors who have overseen images and directed the work of the column's photographers include Lonnie Schlein, Jessica DeWitt, Gina Privitere, Darcy Eveleigh, Laura O'Neill, Chris Jones, and the late John Forbes. The newspaper column's design is the work of the *Times* art director Rodrigo Honeywell.

Among the many editors on the *Times* Travel and Escapes copy desks who have kept "36 Hours" at its best over the years, three who stand out are Florence Stickney, Steve Bailey, and Carl Sommers. Editors of the column on the *New York Times* web site have been Alice Dubois, David Allan, Miki Meek, Allison Busacca, and Danielle Belopotosky. Much of the fact-checking, that most invaluable and unsung of skills, was in the hands of Rusha Haljuci, Nick Kaye, Anna Bahney, and George Gustines.

Finally, we must offer a special acknowledgment to Benedikt Taschen, whose longtime readership and interest in the "36 Hours" column led to the partnership of our two companies to produce this book.

— BARBARA IRELAND AND ALEX WARD

Editor Barbara Ireland
Project management Alex Ward
Photo editor Phyllis Collazo
Maps Natasha Perkel
Spot illustrations and region maps Olimpia Zagnoli
Editorial coordination Nina Wiener and Eric Schwartau
Art direction Marco Zivny and Josh Baker
Layout and design Marco Zivny
Production Jennifer Patrick

To stay informed about upcoming TASCHEN titles, please request our magazine at www.taschen.com/magazine or write to TASCHEN, Hohenzollernring 53, D–50672 Cologne, Germany, contact@taschen.com. We will be happy to send you a free copy of our magazine which is filled with information about all of our books.

© 2013 TASCHEN GmbH
Hohenzollernring 53, D–50672 Köln, www.taschen.com

ISBN 978-3-8365-4201-2 Printed in China

TRUST *THE NEW YORK TIMES* WITH YOUR NEXT 36 HOURS

"An elegant…planning tool and beautifully photographed coffee-table book."

—FORBES.COM, *NEW YORK*

USA & CANADA*
* also available for iPad and iPhone

EUROPE*

LATIN AMERICA & THE CARIBBEAN

ASIA & OCEANIA

USA & CANADA REGION BY REGION

NORTHEAST

SOUTHEAST

MIDWEST & GREAT LAKES

SOUTHWEST & ROCKY MOUNTAINS

WEST COAST

FOR NEWS ON UPCOMING BOOKS IN THIS SERIES, VISIT TASCHEN.COM/36HOURS

Mont
TREMBLANT 142

Montreal 136

122
Burlington

Stowe
118

Lake
Placid 126

Cooperstown
132

NEW LONDON
68

the
Brandywine
Valley 64

NEW YORK
CITY 10

I ♥ NY

East Hampton 4

PHILADELPHIA 58

CAPE
MAY 52

Princeton 46